Euripides: Phoenician Women

BLOOMSBURY COMPANIONS
TO GREEK AND ROMAN TRAGEDY

Series editor: Thomas Harrison

Aeschylus: Agamemnon
Barbara Goward

Aeschylus: Persians
David Rosenbloom

Aeschylus: Seven Against Thebes
Isabelle Torrance

Euripides: Bacchae
Sophie Mills

Euripides: Heracles
Emma Griffiths

Euripides: Hippolytus
Sophie Mills

Euripides: Iphigenia at Aulis
Pantelis Michelakis

Euripides: Medea
William Allan

Euripides: Phoenician Women
Thalia Papadopoulou

Seneca: Phaedra
Roland Mayer

Seneca: Thyestes
P.J. Davis

Sophocles: Ajax
Jon Hesk

Sophocles: Electra
Michael Lloyd

Sophocles: Philoctetes
Hanna M. Roisman

Sophocles: Women of Trachis
Brad Levett

BLOOMSBURY COMPANIONS
TO GREEK AND ROMAN TRAGEDY

Euripides:
Phoenician Women

Thalia Papadopoulou

B L O O M S B U R Y
LONDON • NEW DELHI • NEW YORK • SYDNEY

Bloomsbury Academic
An imprint of Bloomsbury Publishing Plc

50 Bedford Square
London
WC1B 3DP
UK

1385 Broadway
New York
NY 10018
USA

www.bloomsbury.com

**Bloomsbury is a registered trade mark of Bloomsbury
Publishing Plc**

British Library Cataloguing-in-Publication Data
A catalogue record for this book is available from the British Library.

ISBN: PB: 978-0-7156-3464-6
ePDF: 978-1-4725-2127-9
ePUB: 978-1-4725-2128-6

Library of Congress Cataloging-in-Publication Data
A catalog record for this book is available from the Library of Congress.

Contents

For

Mary Mantziou

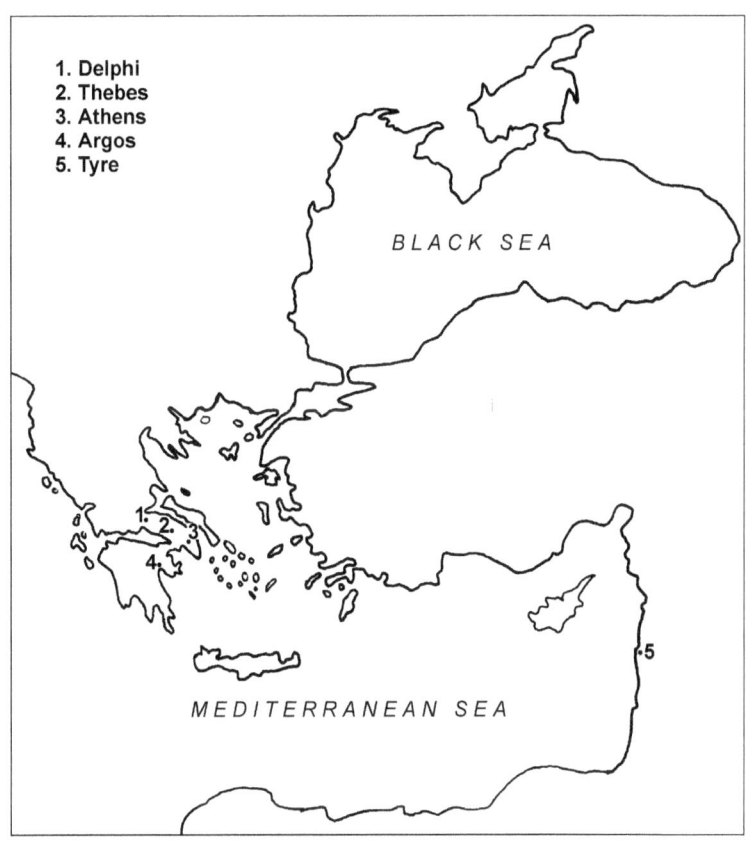

1. Delphi
2. Thebes
3. Athens
4. Argos
5. Tyre

BLACK SEA

MEDITERRANEAN SEA

The world of *Phoenician Women*

Acknowledgements

It is a great pleasure to acknowledge the help I have received during the preparation of the present book. I am grateful to Tom Harrison, Series Editor, Deborah Blake, Editorial Director, the anonymous reader and the staff at Duckworth, for their editorial expertise, constructive assistance and efficient over-seeing of the production of the volume. My deepest thanks are to Pat Easterling for reading earlier drafts and giving acute and valuable advice on a variety of issues, as well as for being a constant source of kindness, encouragement and inspiration. Last but not least, I would like to thank my family and friends, on whom I can always rely.

Preface

Euripides' *Phoenician Women*, one of the latest Euripidean tragedies, is an intriguing play which represents some of Euripides' finest dramatic technique. Rich in cast and varied in incident, it is an example of Euripides' experimentation with structure. It dramatizes the most fertile mythical tradition of the city of Thebes and its doomed royal family, focusing in particular on the conflict between Eteocles and Polynices as a result of their father's Oedipus' curse, which eventually leads to mutual fratricide. The play was very popular throughout antiquity, while it came to be part of the so-called 'Byzantine triad' (along with *Hecuba* and *Orestes*), which was chosen for the school curriculum. This book offers a thorough study of the play in its historical context, against the background of Athenian tragedy and Euripidean dramaturgy. The study, which employs various critical approaches, investigates the literary tradition and the dynamics of intertextuality, characterization, plot-development, the use of rhetoric, gender, the function of the Chorus, aspects of performance and the reception of the play from antiquity to modern times.

References to the Euripidean text follow James Diggle's edition in the Oxford Classical Text series (J. Diggle 1994, *Euripides Fabulae: Tomus III*. Oxford: Clarendon Press). For passages suspected for interpolation several other editions have been taken into account, esp. D.J. Mastronarde 1994, *Euripides: Phoenissae*. Cambridge: Cambridge UP. Translations of Euripides' *Phoenician Women* are quoted from E. Craik 1988, *Euripides: Phoenician Women*. Warminster: Aris & Phillips (Oxbow). Translations of other texts, unless otherwise stated, are mine. Dates of most authors and their works are given in the Chronology. The following abbreviations of book titles have been used:

Davies = M. Davies (1988), *Epicorum Graecorum fragmenta*. Göttingen: Vandenhoeck and Ruprecht.

D-K = H. Diels and W. Kranz (1952), *Fragmente der Vorsokratiker*, 6th edn Berlin: Wiedmann.

FGrH = F. Jacoby (1923-58), *Die Fragmente der griechischen Historiken*. Leiden: Brill.

K-A = R. Kassel and C. Austin (1984), *Poetae comici Graeci*, vol. iii 2: *Aristophanes: Testimonia et fragmenta*. Berlin and New York: Walter De Gruyter.

LIMC = *Lexicon Iconographicum Mythologiae Classicae* (9 vols in 18 parts, 1981-99). Zurich: Artemis Verlag.

M-W = R. Merkelbach and M.L. West (1968), *Fragmenta Hesiodea*. Oxford: Oxford UP.

PMGF = M. Davies (1991), *Poetarum melicorum Graecorum fragmenta*. Oxford: Oxford UP.

TrGF = R. Kannicht (2004), *Tragicorum Graecorum Fragmenta*, vol. 5: *Euripides*. Göttingen: Vandenhoeck and Ruprecht.

West = M.L. West (1992²), *Iambi et elegi Graeci ante Alexandri cantati*. Oxford: Oxford UP.

Information about modern productions of Euripides' *Phoenician Women* has mostly been collected on-line from two databases: *The Archive of Performances of Greek and Roman Drama* (Oxford University, www.apgrd.ox.ac.uk) and *The Reception of the Texts and Images of Ancient Greece in Late Twentieth-Century Drama and Poetry in English* (The Open University, www2.open.ac.uk/ClassicalStudies/GreekPlays).

1
Poet and Play

Euripides and his world

Euripides,[1] from the Attic deme of Phlya, was the youngest of the three great tragic playwrights and, arguably, the most controversial. He was born between 485 and 480 BC and died in 407/6 in Macedon,[2] at the court of king Archelaus. The period in which he lived was a time of radical change in Athens. The Athenian state, in charge of the Delian League, gradually turned the alliance into an empire and its allies into subjects. It became a cultural centre where many intellectuals came to settle. But the Peloponnesian War, which forms the background of most of Euripides' surviving plays, also marked the beginning of a crisis, from which Athens made a fair recovery in the 4th century. There was, then, a gradual process from Athens' grandeur to devastation that Euripides witnessed in his own time and reflected in various ways in his dramas.

What has come down to us regarding Euripides' life and career[3] consists in an ancient *Life*, an entry in the Byzantine *Suda*, fragments of a *Life of Euripides* by Satyrus, a chapter by Aulus Gellius in his *Attic Nights*, a brief biography by Thomas Magister and a collection of five epistles which are said to have been written by the poet but are dated in the second century AD.[4] Information about his life and career is of varying credibility, often unreliable and surrounded by fantasy or influenced by comic parody. Thus for example the detail that his mother sold vegetables in the market, which is recorded in his biography, is also a recurrent joke in Aristophanes (e.g. *Women at the Thesmophoria*, 387). His ancient *Life* states that Euripides'

11

own experience of the immoral behaviour of his wife was the reason that made him compose his first *Hippolytus*. Tradition also reported that he lived in isolation in a cave on Salamis and that he owned a good library. In both these cases what is pointed out is the alleged reclusiveness of an artist as well as his erudition, which is evident in his plays. Euripides' erudition is relevant to his attitude to religion and philosophy; he was prosecuted for impiety by the demagogue Cleon and allegedly had close acquaintance with leading thinkers,[5] whose doctrines often caused them to be suspected of atheism. The exact truth of whether he was in fact a close associate of theirs eludes us, but, in a wider context, again what we are faced with may be the merging of a dramatist's work with his actual life. This is after all a common mistake in ancient biographies, where views expressed by characters in dramas are not evaluated in context but are identified with the views of the dramatist himself. It is not surprising, then, that Euripides was known in antiquity as 'the philosopher from the stage' (as if his primary task was to write philosophy and not literature) and also considered seriously as a philosopher, as becomes evident from the numerous quotations from his dramas in philosophical works from Aristotle down to Cicero. In all these examples, it seems that Euripides exhibits in his works qualities that are shared by sophists and philosophers, namely a critical and inquiring mind which is willing to question conventional truths and given assumptions.[6]

Euripides' first dramatic production, which included the *Daughters of Pelias*, is recorded in 455 BC. His début earned him the third prize. We have ninety-two titles of his works, out of which eighteen tragedies and one satyr-play (*Cyclops*) survive complete.[7] Among his extant tragedies *Alcestis*, which is the earliest (438), was performed in the dramatic contest in the place of a satyr drama; it has often been regarded as quasi-satyric but should rather be treated as an early example of Euripides' innovation and experimentation with dramatic form. In other words, in *Alcestis* Euripides explores the possibilities of a tragedy which is informed by and evokes to the audience elements familiar from satyr-drama. One of the nineteen plays, *Rhesus*, though attributed to Euripides in the manuscript tradition, is thought by most scholars nowadays to be by a fourth-century dramatist. We are fortunate too in that several fragments of other plays, some of great length, have survived and give a good idea of Euripides' dramatic technique. Although he produced many plays, Euripides won only four victories in his lifetime along with a posthumous victory through his son with *Iphigenia at Aulis* and *Bacchae*.[8] The record of his victories, compared to that of Aeschylus (thirteen) and Sophocles (eighteen) shows that he was not very successful during the dramatic competitions, though the fact that he was granted a Chorus to contest at the Dionysia shows that his dramatic art was appreciated by his contemporaries. It was after his death, especially from the fourth century onwards, that he reached great popularity.[9] Aristotle, in his *Poetics* (1453a29), famously called him the 'tragic poet par excellence', which has often been taken to mean expertise in arousing the tragic emotions of pity and fear. As a result of his popularity in antiquity and in the Byzantine period, as well as owing to luck, there have been more of his plays preserved than the seven plays by each of Aeschylus and Sophocles.

Euripides is often considered as an innovator. This becomes evident in many of his dramatic treatments, where he is often bold in deviating from other versions of the myth and in surprising his audience with sudden twists in the plots. As dramatists normally drew from the repository of heroic saga, each one attempted to differentiate his own treatment from earlier ones and guide the audience's reception by relying on their familiarity with earlier versions and introducing changes. Sometimes his innovations are made in a self-conscious way and Euripides engages in a dialogue with previous treatments by other tragic playwrights: the recognition between Orestes and Electra in *Electra* is a prime example of intertextuality in which Euripides parodies the supposed naïveté of the same scene in Aeschylus' *Libation-Bearers* (where the recognition is made simply by a lock of hair, a footprint and a piece of clothing). This is a famous instance, in fact, where intertextuality almost amounts to a suspension of dramatic illusion (by convention this is explicitly done only in comedy).[10]

Another aspect of Euripides' innovations with regard to plot partly contributed to his popularity in subsequent times: especially in some of his late plays (*Iphigenia among the Taurians, Helen, Ion*), he showed a great preference for plots involving an increasing element of intrigue, mistaken identity, recognition, rescue, divine help, often resulting in happy endings. At the same time, the exotic atmosphere of some plays and the suggested wish for escape from a world of hardship at a time when Athens, involved in the Peloponnesian War, had begun to show alarming signs of decadence, made the character of these plays distinct. The happy ending, in particular, has often puzzled critics, who called them tragi-comic, melodramatic or romantic.[11] As in subsequent times New Comedy and Roman Comedy often based their complex plots on themes such as intrigue, mistaken identity and happy reunions, it is understandable why audiences of these later times largely enjoyed Euripidean plays. With regard to Euripides himself, his liking for such plots indicates again, as in the case of *Alcestis*, his experimentation with the tragic genre and his wish to pursue the potentiality for a sort of tragedy which breaks new ground. It is not surprising, then, that humorous and comic elements abound in Euripidean plays and often introduce a deeply ironic perspective.[12] Instead of being regarded as alien, they are better understood as conscious experimentations with the capacity of the tragic genre to incorporate elements intrinsic to other genres.

Euripides' innovation with characters and his preference for realism were noted in antiquity. Aristophanes parodied this tendency especially in his *Frogs*, where Euripides is accused of opting for ordinary and unheroic characters rather than the traditional heroic figures that Aeschylus portrayed. Aristotle in his *Poetics* (1460b33) quoted Sophocles as saying that he himself portrayed men as they should be whereas Euripides as they actually are. The atmosphere of Euripides' dramas seems

14

indeed realistic and his characters often seem closer to everyday people than to the heroes they represent. It is true that an increased sense of realism reduces the distance between the heroic world of saga and the reality of the audience and makes it easier to filter the dramatic world through fifth-century concerns. Sometimes, however, this is carried to extremes, as in *Orestes*, where Euripides strips the heroes of any grandeur, displays their failure in achieving any heroic status and depicts a moral anarchy and bleak corruption on the verge of nihilism; this must have seemed particularly alarming to the audience watching the play in 408 (soon before the defeat of Athens) and possibly living in fear of discord and breakdown in their own city. Even in cases when they are unnamed, they become vital for the forwarding of the plot. For example, in *Hippolytus* the Nurse is given a decisive part in the plot; in *Orestes* the Messenger part is given to a Phrygian slave who sings his part in dialect and adds a comic touch to an otherwise gloomy tragedy.[13]

Euripides shows a great interest in the motivation of his characters and often turns the focus inwards to suggest his characters' innermost thoughts and intimate feelings. In antiquity he was famous for his skill in depicting in particular two central emotional states, namely, madness and love.[14] In modern terms he would be called a master of human psychology.[15] In *Medea* he shows his heroine torn between her maternal love and her wish for revenge. *Hecuba* and *Ion* also provide him with a unique opportunity to explore female psychology under various circumstances which display affection as well as revenge. In *Hippolytus* he explores human sexuality and the disastrous aftermaths of its suppression. In his versions of Orestes' matricide in *Electra* and *Orestes* he gives the impression of providing the audience with a direct presentation of the heroes' personality.

Women[16] have a prominent role in Euripides, and their portrayal has caused contradictory reactions since antiquity, sometimes including oversimplistic views such as the accusation of misogyny. Perhaps the most famous example is

Aristophanes' *Women at the Thesmophoria*, a comedy whose very subject-matter is a women's assembly at Athens which decides to put a drastic end to Euripides' attacks on the female species in his plays. Aristophanes often parodied the Euripidean portrayals of supposedly 'bad women' in his tragedies (*Frogs* 1078-82). Such portrayals of immoral or violent women were not of course a Euripidean feature alone, especially if one thinks of the Aeschylean Clytemnestra, the tragic 'prototype'. What happens in Euripides is that he obviously tries to make his heroines sympathetic to the audience by showing the circumstances and motives behind their actions. In doing so, Euripides makes excellent use of the rhetorical techniques of his time,[17] giving his heroines persuasive arguments to support their cases. This was certainly not entirely new in tragedy; the difference is that these arguments no longer reflect traditional assumptions about the role of women but seem to undermine them; thus, for example, the Nurse in *Hippolytus* uses argument to support the view that female adultery is not wrong. There are also examples where Euripides is considered to be a feminist, as in cases where he gives voice to the female reaction against male censure of women (e.g. Euripides, *Medea* 416-30; *Ion* 1090-8; *TrGF* 494 (the *Captive Melanippe*)). Euripides became famous for the portrayals especially of controversial female characters, but in his plays there is a wide range of female portraits, including honourable mothers and queens (e.g. Aethra in *Suppliants*), wise priestesses (e.g. Theonoe in *Helen*), or courageous virgins (e.g. Macaria in *Children of Heracles*).

Euripides' treatment of war and of the gods is also contested by critics. Some of his plays (notably *Suppliants* and *Children of Heracles*) are clearly patriotic in tone in the sense of praising the grandeur of Athens as the powerful city which upholds justice and supports the weak.[18] What Euripides stresses is that war should be fought only when the cause is just. In several other plays, with *Trojan Women* being the prime example,[19] his use of myth reveals the dire consequences of the politics of expansionism for any city, like Athens, that achieves hegemony and abuses her power. In general, Euripides explores the validity and limits of all assertions made by his contemporaries regarding their polis and their relations with other states. Even the established dichotomy between the categories 'Greek' and 'barbarian' becomes a means by which he reveals the failure of given presuppositions and cautions against transgression of limits.[20]

In the case of the gods in his plays,[21] Euripides shows both vindictive gods who may be criticized by humans for their ferocity (e.g. Dionysus in *Bacchae* and Aphrodite in *Hippolytus*) and benevolent gods (e.g. Athena in *Iphigenia among the Taurians*), while he often seems to attack the anthropomorphic deities of tradition and blend philosophical trends with established religion. He has often been regarded as interested in the history of religion, as several of his plays contain cultic aetiology, namely, they explain contemporary cult by linking it to myth, but he has also been seen as a critic of traditional gods whose plays undermine traditional religion. Again, the great variety which characterizes the religious universe of Euripides' dramas should caution against simplistic approaches which run the risk of ignoring the context and substituting the playwright's own beliefs for characters' views. Euripides is surely influenced by sceptics regarding religion and by philosophers of his time but he is working on the fabric of myth, which presupposes the existence of anthropomorphic gods. What he does is to explore divine presence with regard to human life and mankind's expectations of their gods. Euripides shows that reciprocity is an important issue, which humans hope for but cannot guarantee. Above all, he draws his audience's attention to the gap between gods and mortals and the difficulty that humans have in understanding divine workings no matter how hard they try.

Emotion and rhetoric are two areas which show Euripidean skill and variety though they have sometimes been considered difficult to reconcile. Euripides' plays abound in emotional outbursts, as evident in his frequent use of monodies and lyric exchanges as well as in his employment of innovative rhythms under the influence of the musical developments of his time,[22] in order to convey the innermost emotional turmoil of his characters. On the other hand, he was an expert in providing his characters with effective arguments to argue and counterargue a case. This expertise in oratorical skills has sometimes been found stylized and frigid to the extent of stripping characters of emotion and substituting set-piece arguments for round characterization. What is often forgotten in this case is the high degree of the audience's familiarity with debates and all types of argumentation in their everyday life, from the assembly to the lawcourts. Speech, argumentation and debates have a prominent role in Euripides and show the fertile influence of contemporary rhetoric. But they are not devoid of emotion; rather, in each case they should be contextualized in order to reveal their contribution to characterization and to the main thematic concerns.

Overall, Euripides was a dramatist whose very versatility has caused contradictory remarks since antiquity:[23] he has been considered a misogynist but also a feminist; an atheist but also a man of religious beliefs; a defender of Athens' foreign policies but also an advocate of anti-war propaganda; a master of character delineation but also fond of rhetoric to the extent of undermining character. He was, too, a restless mind, open to all intellectual developments of his time. His dramas display an awareness of contemporary theories in every field of knowledge, including moral philosophy and philosophy of language, political and rhetorical theory, and music, as well as sciences such as medicine[24] or cosmology. His dramatization of myths constantly explores political and ethical issues, always in a way which gives the primary role to the audience. It is not accidental, then, that his plays so often trigger different responses by audiences and critics alike; even in cases where closure seems to be effected by the divine appearances at the end, a typical Euripidean ending, the major issues often remain open and invite the audience to make judgements and articulate their own opinions.

The play: synopsis and plot

Phoenician Women is set in Thebes and treats aspects of the troubled house of Oedipus and his descendants. The *prologos* ('prologue'), namely, the part prior to the entry of the Chorus, is divided into a monologue (1-87), a typical Euripidean feature, by Jocasta and an exchange between the young Antigone and a Tutor (*paidagogos*) (88-201). Jocasta identifies herself, reviews the past and describes the present situation to the audience. The mood is that of urgency, as her son Polynices has arrived with an army to demand his share in his ancestral land from his brother Eteocles. Her speech ends with an invocation to Zeus to save them and grant reconciliation. Following her exit, Antigone and an old Tutor appear on the top of the *skênê*, representing the palace roof, and are engaged in a lyric dialogue, where Antigone asks questions about the invaders and the Tutor informs her about their identities. This scene recalls the famous Teichoskopia ('viewing from the walls') in *Iliad* 3, where the two interlocutors were Priam and Helen.

Following the *prologos* comes the *parodos* (202-60), namely the entry of the fifteen young women of the Chorus. Their identity must have been known to the audience from the very title of the play, but their exact relation to Thebes and the dramatic situation must have kept the audience in suspense. They are foreigners who have been trapped in the siege of Thebes on their journey from Phoenicia to Delphi. At the same time they stress that their origins, as descendants of Agenor, tie them with the origins of Cadmus, the founder of Thebes. Thus, the Chorus are presented as both detached (non Theban citizens) and close (tied by kinship) to the Thebans; their attitude is clearly one of concern for the plight that has befallen the city.

The Choral song ends with Polynices' entry, which opens the (unusually long) first episode of the play (261-637). Following an exchange between Polynices and the Chorus (261-95), Jocasta appears again to greet her son in an emotional outburst, which mingles joy at Polynices' return and grief at his long absence (301-54). Their ensuing dialogue displays

Polynices' nostalgia as well as his resentment for the injustice he has suffered and soon takes the form of a line-by-line exchange, where Polynices informs his mother about his life after he left Thebes. The next scene of the episode (443-587) starts with the arrival of Eteocles and dramatizes an *agôn* (debate) between the two brothers before their mother, who acts as the arbitrator. Setting up *agôn* scenes is a recurrent feature in Euripidean drama, which shows the influence of rhetoric as well as the audience's interest in displays of oratorical skills. Polynices insists that justice is on his side, namely, Eteocles has done him wrong by violating his agreement to allow his brother to rule Thebes in turn, while Eteocles defends himself by appealing to the relativism of all ideas and stresses that he would do anything to possess what he considers to be the greatest good, that is, monarchy. Jocasta's response is an address to each of her sons in turn in an attempt to dissuade them from their course of action. Her long speech, which makes a powerful case for equity and justice, is followed by the Chorus' appeal to the gods to bring reconciliation (586-7). The last part of the first episode (588-637) is an even more intense and harsh exchange between the two brothers, which leaves no room at all for reconciliation.

The first *stasimon* (638-89) shows the urgency of the situation and reveals the Chorus' concern for the city. They sing of the archetypal myth of Thebes, namely, the arrival of Cadmus and his settlement, following the killing of Ares' dragon according to Apollo's oracle. The reference to Apollo is linked with the identification of the place (642-3), and the sowing of the dragon's teeth is associated with Athena (666-7). Violence and calm are elements that characterize the myth and give the tone of this ode, which piously invokes the protecting deities of Thebes, as well as Epaphus, the common ancestor of both Phoenicians and Thebans, to save Thebes and avert disaster.

In the brief second episode (690-783) Eteocles converses with his uncle Creon and decides to follow his advice regarding the plan of defence to be followed. This scene anticipates the duel of the two brothers (754-6). It also anticipates later developments, including the marriage of Antigone and Haemon, the consultation of Tiresias and the refusal of burial to the body of Polynices, all of which are Eteocles' requests to Creon. In the second *stasimon* (784-832), the Chorus invoke the gods and refer to the past (both recent and remote) in a manner which invests the dramatic present too with a sinister tone.

The entry of Tiresias in the third episode (834-1018), expected from Eteocles' words in the second episode, brings an unexpected twist in the plot. Following an account of past events and a foretelling of the brothers' imminent death, he finally reveals to Creon with reluctance that according to gods' will the safety of Thebes requires the sacrifice of Menoeceus, Creon's own son (911-14). Creon's offensive response prompts the prophet to explain that the gods demand the sacrifice of Menoeceus so that the anger of Ares at Cadmus' killing of the dragon can be propitiated. Creon attempts to save his son by sending him away from Thebes, but Menoeceus causes another twist in the plot by deceiving his father, sending him offstage and expressing his determination to be sacrificed for the sake of Thebes (991-1018). The third *stasimon* (1019-66) is largely concerned with the Sphinx and her killing by Oedipus, who saved the city of Thebes. The Chorus briefly refer to the sacrifice of Menoeceus (1054-9) in a way which gives him in the present the role of the saviour that Oedipus had in the past. A hopeful note seems to be struck here, but it is at once undermined, as the mention of Oedipus recalls all the horror he brought with him. There is, then, a tone of frustrated optimism and an ominous sense that the royal family of Thebes cannot escape from her troubles.

The fourth episode (1067-283) contains two long Messenger speeches: the first (1090-199) is a description of the enemy and the battle, while the second (1217-63) focuses on the meeting of the two brothers and calls for Jocasta's intercession to prevent the worst. The episode concludes with Jocasta and Antigone both leaving urgently to meet the two brothers on the battlefield. Their exit is followed by the fourth *stasimon* (1284-306), a brief ode which has the character of a dirge, as the Chorus lament in advance the mutual death of the two brothers, which they now consider inescapable.

Following the last *stasimon* is the *exodos*,[25] namely, the final scene of the play, which is divided into three parts: the first (1308-479) opens with the entry of Creon, who laments for his son and is anxious to hear about Jocasta, then follows with a long messenger speech, divided into two sections by a choral couplet (1425-6). The first part of the speech (1356-424) describes the duel between Eteocles and Polynices, while the second (1427-79) recounts the mutual fratricide and the suicide of Jocasta over the corpses of her sons. The next part of the *exodos* (1480-581) includes Antigone's dirge over the three corpses that have been carried onstage, followed by Oedipus' appearance, which comes as a surprise: He emerges from the palace, where he had been confined by his sons, to hear the news of the deaths and join Antigone in lyric exchange. In the last part of the *exodos* (1582-766), whose authenticity has been a debatable issue, Creon, now ruler of the country, announces the future exile of Oedipus, whose curse on his sons began their strife, the future marriage of Antigone and Haemon and the refusal of burial to the corpse of Polynices. These orders and Oedipus' speech of despair are followed by an exchange in which Antigone defies Creon's orders and asserts her willingness to bury Polynices' body, refuse marriage and accompany her father into exile. The play ends with Antigone and her aged father in a lyric duet, sorrowfully departing in exile.

As the above synopsis shows, the play is particularly rich in both character and incident. Its design is an excellent example of an 'open' as opposed to a 'closed' structure, namely it relies on a multiplication of both character and episode.[26] These elements apparently attracted the interest of ancient scholiasts and were noted in two of the ancient prefaces (*hypotheseis*) to the play: this tragedy is called *poluprosôpon*, that is, it has many characters, and *paraplêrômatikon*, that is, 'overfull', a word which probably implies the great proportion of dramatic scenes which are not necessarily causally related. The plot does not unfold in a linear manner or in a clear sequence of dramatic events but is based on self-contained, episodic scenes. There is no central character to dominate the dramatic action from the beginning to the end, but different characters play prominent and crucial parts in different sections. There are events which are given importance but whose exact relation to the main dramatic action invites speculation. Such is the function of the Menoeceus scene, peripheral to its main plot, but making an intriguing contribution to the play's thematic concerns. Time too is not sequential, but the past constantly interrupts and informs the dramatic present in a way suggestive of the inter-linking of events as well as of the recurrence of similar sequences. Causal connection is not invalidated but is greatly enriched by parallels and contrasts that the audience are constantly invited to think about.

Date and transmission of text[27]

There is no certain date for the *Phoenician Women* preserved in the ancient prefaces to the play or in other sources, but there is some information which helps us establish an approximate date.[28] A scholium (ancient comment) on l. 53 of Aristophanes' *Frogs*, produced at the Lenaea of 405, asks why Aristophanes chose to mention *Andromeda* (produced in 412) and not for example *Hypsipyle*, *Phoenician Women* or *Antiope*, which were more recent.[29] On the basis of this evidence, a date between 411 and 407 (Euripides' death) should be sought. We know that Euripides left for Macedon soon after the production of his *Orestes* in 408, so a date between 411 and 409 seems more possible. A date in 409 would be closer to the production of the *Frogs*. On the other hand, there are two factors which may also be considered. The political language of the play has often been taken as alluding to the turmoil leading to the oligarchic revo-lution at Athens in 411 and to the figure of Alcibiades. In particular 411 was the year in which the recall of Alcibiades from exile was decreed by the army at Samos and ratified, following the fall of the Four Hundred, by the Athenian assembly (Thucydides 8.81.97). This may be valid but it can hardly help in fixing the precise year of production. The other type of evidence used for finding approximate dates for undated Euripidean plays is metrical, based on the observation that when the securely dated plays of Euripides are arranged chronologically what is noted is a clear tendency towards more freedom in the structure of the iambic trimeter, which involves more resolutions. On this criterion the *Phoenician Women* is most comparable to *Helen* (produced in 412). Be that as it may, the period of 411 to 409 remains the most plausible for dating the production of the *Phoenician Women*.

The problem of interpolation in ancient texts has been a puzzling issue since antiquity and an especially persistent one in the case of the *Phoenician Women*.[30] Ancient critics have on occasion remarked that some parts are not genuine and have been followed by modern scholars who have deleted what each considered not authentic, from single lines to entire scenes. The scenes that have caused the greatest suspicion are the Teichoskopia scene between Antigone and the Tutor and especially the final scene between Antigone and her father. Interpolation is a major issue of textual criticism, which attempts to establish a version of text as close as possible to the author's original. Especially during the nineteenth century there was a great confidence among textual critics in the possibility of 'recovering' the authorial version and a strong tendency to intervene drastically in the text and delete whatever seemed suspect. In recent years critics tend to be more conservative, especially in cases where passages are suspect in terms of consistency or coherence.

In the case of Euripides' original text, the script must have been written in capital letters, with no separations between words and no distinction in the layout of lyric and dialogue parts. The idea of text in the period in which Euripides composed his plays was fluid and not fixed. Copies were probably circulated only among the performers of each production, while more copies could be made later for the reading public. In the late fourth century the politician Lycurgus passed a decree which dictated that performances of the plays by the then canonical playwrights, namely, Aeschylus, Sophocles and Euripides, had to conform to the original texts. The need for such measure was due to the frequent alterations made, especially by actors who added sections to embellish their parts.[31] For this reason, an 'official' text of the plays was prepared and established.

The second important phase towards standardizing ancient texts came in the third century with the work of Alexandrian scholars, which laid the foundations of philological criticism. The Library of Alexandria provided a unique centre for collecting the material, making comparative analysis and editing texts. Aristophanes of Byzantium in particular is credited with making editions of all the plays by Aeschylus, Sophocles and Euripides which had survived in his time. His hypothesis to the *Phoenician Women* has survived in the manuscripts but in a fragmentary form, while the corpus of the scholia on the *Phoenician Women* contains various ancient comments, many of them anonymous but some attributed to known Alexandrian scholars. Copies of the texts established by the Alexandrian scholars were circulated and multiplied throughout antiquity and Byzantine times.

The transmission of the Euripidean text includes two manuscript traditions: One manuscript (L) has preserved nine plays in alphabetical order from Epsilon to Kappa (so *Helen* and Cyclops (*Kyklops*) were preserved) and adds to another tradition which has preserved a total of ten plays chosen in antiquity as Euripides' 'select' plays in the same manner that seven were chosen from each of Aeschylus and Sophocles. Not only was the *Phoenician Women* part of this ancient canon,[32] a fact that attests its popularity, but it was also one of the three plays (with *Hecuba* and *Orestes*) that formed the so-called 'Byzantine triad' of the most popular tragedies. This selection, which probably had to do with educational concerns and preferences, also led to an increasing study of these plays, which, as a result, have been transmitted along with a great number of commentaries. The play has the richest scholia and its wealth of good ideas as noticed by the ancient hypothesis may have contributed to its proliferation (see further Chapter 6). From the sixth century AD, and especially after the closing of the Academy at Athens by emperor Justinian, came a long period of hostility towards paganism, which threatened the survival of the ancient texts. It was only in the ninth century AD that this was reversed, as this period, with the upsurge of classical learning, was a crucial time for the recovery of ancient tradition. This fortunate change promoted the production and dissemination of manuscripts and helped preserve a majority of texts which would have otherwise been doomed to perish. The advent of print in the subsequent centuries revolutionized the transmission of all written texts; the first printed edition of the *Phoenician Women* (the Aldine edition) was made in Venice in 1503 and was followed by a long tradition of manuscript collations, critical observations on interpolation and critical editions of the text up to the present, especially by Diggle (Oxford Classical Texts) and Mastronarde (Teubner).[33]

2
Myth and Intertextuality

The corpus of Greek myths was the revered transmitter of a collective cultural identity in ancient Greece, which provided a link with the legendary past and an affirmation of a valid heritage. The transmission of these myths involved preservation and new synthesis. Although the majority of the myth cycles and their genealogical and chronological arrangement seem to have been broadly established by the seventh century, each literary creation was free to introduce variations. Greek tragedy drew heavily for its subject-matter from pre-existing literature, especially from epic and lyric poetry, in a creative way which reshaped the inherited myth to make it relevant to the contemporary reality of its spectators.[1] Since it was coined in the 1960s by the semiotician J. Kristeva, the term intertextuality has become a dominant idea in literary criticism.[2] It has broken with traditional notions of 'sources', 'influences' or 'authorial intentions' and drawn attention to the fact that a text is not self-sufficient but a complex signifying system, whose meaning emerges from its various relations to other texts. The texts which precede, underlie and are modified and elaborated by any given text are its subtexts (or hypotexts). Since dramatists wrote plays in which their version of a myth relied on their audience's familiarity with the wider repertoire of myth, it is evident that the intertextual process involves not only the framing of texts by other texts, but also the framing of the audience's perception and lived experience by other texts. Intertextuality has a prominent part in Euripides' *Phoenician Women* and it is interesting to see the attitude of the play towards earlier versions of the myth.

The *Phoenician Women* draws from the Theban cycle[3] and treats one of the major motifs in Greek tragedy, namely, familial crisis. Its main subject matter is the strife and eventual fratricide of Oedipus' sons, Eteocles and Polynices. This fratricide is one of the final ramifications of a long family crisis within the troubled royal house of Thebes, which spans three generations, starting from Laius, Oedipus' father. Epic and lyric poetry treated several aspects of the myth. The marriage of Oedipus with his mother Epicaste (a variant name of Jocasta) is mentioned in the *Odyssey* (11.271-80), along with Epicaste's suicide by hanging and Oedipus' distress, but there is no reference to their offspring. Pausanias, on the basis of Homer's *Odyssey* and the epic *Oedipodia*, argued (9.5.11) that Oedipus and Jocasta had no children and that the mother of Eteocles, Polynices, Antigone and Ismene was Eurygania, Oedipus' second wife. He also mentions a painting by Onasias at Plataea (the date is unknown), where Eurygania is the woman who grieves during her sons' fight. The ancient scholia on Euripides' *Phoenician Women* report similar views by the early epic poet Pisander (scholium on Euripides' *Phoenician Women* 1760) and the mythographer Pherecydes (scholium on Euripides' *Phoenician Women* 53), namely, that the mother of Oedipus' four children was Eurygania and not Jocasta, though Pherecydes also writes that Oedipus and Jocasta had two sons, Phrastor and Laonytus.[4] All tragic versions assume incestuous offspring by Oedipus and Jocasta; the earliest known occurrence would be Aeschylus' *Seven against Thebes* (752-7). The offspring of an incestuous union may be said to convey a sort of horror which is suitable for tragic treatment. Conversely, the epic treatments, such as in Homer, which do not mention this may reflect either ignorance or conscious silence for the sake of propriety (*decorum*). As for the mention of a non-incestuous wife of Oedipus in later versions, it may have been the result of an attempt by families who traced their origin in Polynices at removing incest from their lineage.[5]

Homer's *Iliad* is familiar with the expedition against Thebes and its siege by Polynices in charge of an army where Tydeus

2. Myth and Intertextuality

has a central role. The references to the siege of Thebes in the *Iliad* (4.378-410, 6.222, 10.285-90), where Diomedes, Tydeus' son, has a prominent role, are exemplary and paradigmatic: they are meant to create an antecedent to the siege of Troy by linking the present to the familiar heroic exploit of a previous generation. Apart from Homer, several aspects of the myth of Thebes, including the riddle of Sphinx and the expedition against Thebes, are briefly mentioned in Hesiod's *Theogony* (326) and *Works and Days* (162). In the latter epic the expedition of the Seven and the siege of Troy are mentioned as two great heroic exploits. Other epics, now known by name or fragmentary but extant in Euripides' time, including *Oedipodia* and *Thebaid*, treated certain episodes of Theban myth.[6] The *Thebaid* in particular, as the opening line shows, started with the expedition against Thebes and was probably entirely focused on this subject. The Theban cycle was the inspiration for a number of other tragedies besides the *Phoenician Women*. Those which are now extant are Aeschylus' *Seven against Thebes* (467), Sophocles' *Antigone* (c. 443), *Oedipus the King* (c. 428), *Oedipus at Colonus* (401, posthumously) and Euripides' *Suppliants* (c. 423), while other tragedies, which have survived in fragmentary form, include Aeschylus' *Laius* and *Oedipus*, Sophocles' *Eriphyle*, Euripides' *Antigone*, *Antiope*, *Chrysippus* and *Oedipus*.

Not all literary sources have survived, and the extent of Euripides' innovation in his *Phoenician Women* can be determined only up to a point, by comparison with extant versions of the myth from epic, lyric and tragedy. Where no comparison is possible, Euripides' treatment may follow some non-extant source or may be his own. Jocasta's appearance in the *Phoenician Women* comes as a surprise when one thinks that in Homer (*Odyssey* 11.277-9), Aeschylus (*Seven against Thebes*) and Sophocles (*Oedipus The King* and *Antigone*) Oedipus' wife commits suicide when the identity of her husband and their incest are revealed. But although Jocasta's suicide following the discovery of the incest seems canonical, her survival in Euripides may not be an innovation, as the mediation of Eteocles and Polynices' mother to resolve their quarrel is known from a fifth-century poem, preserved on the Lille papyrus of the second century and attributed to Stesichorus.[7] In Stesichorus the name of the mother does not survive and there is the possibility that the lyric poet presented not the incestuous Jocasta (or the epic variant Epicaste) but Eurygania as the mother of the two brothers.[8] As the brothers in Stesichorus try to avert a dire prophecy given by Tiresias about their fate, the situation is different from the one dramatized by Euripides, although they may seem to share some *topoi* (common elements).[9] At all events, the very idea of the sons' mother intervening and giving them advice aimed at reconciliation may have been a subtext for the central role given to Jocasta by Euripides. In Euripides' *Oedipus*, a fragmentary play which is considered close in date (415-10 BC)[10] to *Phoenician Women*, Jocasta survives the discovery of the incest and expresses her determination to support Oedipus. Both in Euripides' *Oedipus* and in *Phoenician Women* Jocasta has a prominent role, and if *Oedipus* predates *Phoenician Women*, Antigone's reference (*Phoenician Women* 1549-50) to Jocasta tending Oedipus in the past may recall Jocasta's support to Oedipus in *Oedipus*.[11]

The presentation of Antigone relies on the spectators' familiarity with her courage and devotion to familial and moral values in Sophocles' famous play. Sophocles' *Antigone* presents her in a defiant role, in which she chooses to ignore a state decree in order to bury Polynices. Her determination is emphasized further by comparison with her sister Ismene, who acts as a foil. She is also a young person, soon to be married to Haemon, but chooses to uphold her values at the expense of her life. Her defiant devotion to Polynices is a characteristic also of the final scene of Aeschylus' *Seven against Thebes*, which has strong similarities with Euripides' *Phoenician Women* and has been suspected as a later addition under the influence of Sophocles.[12] Although in these versions Antigone dies in Thebes and her courage is evident in her devotion to her brother, in Euripides' *Phoenician Women* and in Sophocles' *Oedipus at Colonus* the theme of her exile is linked to her devotion to her father.

Creon is also familiar as the brother of Jocasta and variously portrayed as the person who ruled Thebes when the royal family of Laius was left without a successor. In Sophocles' *Antigone* Haemon is presented as his last son while there are references to another son, Megareus, who has already died (1303). Aeschylus mentions Megareus as the name of one of the seven defenders of the Theban Gates (*Seven against Thebes* 474). In *Phoenician Women* Haemon is already married and Creon's last son is Menoeceus (942), who is idealized as the one who sacrifices his life for the sake of his city following Tiresias' prophecy. In Sophocles' *Antigone* too there are several hints which connect Megareus' death with the safety of Thebes after Tiresias' prediction (993-5, 1058, 1302-3, 1312-13). There are similarities between the two stories but whether the Sophoclean Megareus and the Euripidean Menoeceus are the same person (as the scholium on *Phoenician Women* 988 assumes) is questionable.[13] Euripides adapts the motif of (self-) sacrifice for the safety of one's city to the dramatic aims of his play and introduces a character who seems to be his own creation. Even his name, Menoeceus, is the same as that of his grandfather (cf. Sophocles' *Antigone* 211) in a way which links this new character firmly to his family tree.[14] Menoeceus' self-abnegation functions as the counterpoint to the two brothers' egoism, and his self-sacrifice in order to guarantee the safety of the city is Euripides' response to the Aeschylean version, where the safety of the city is in Eteocles' hands. Another innovation in the *Phoenician Women* is that Creon's wife, Eurydice, who commits suicide at the end of Sophocles' *Antigone*, is said to have died when Menoeceus was an infant. This detail is crucial, as Euripides introduces a strong bond between Menoeceus and Jocasta, who becomes a mother-figure for her nephew.

Tiresias is the well-known prophet whose predictions, wisdom and intermediary role between gods and humans give him an important role in different phases of the royal house of Thebes. An interesting feature is that he does not come into Aeschylus' *Seven against Thebes* whereas in the *Phoenician Women* Euripides gives him an important part, reminiscent of his role in Stesichorus as well in Sophocles. The scene in the third episode between Tiresias and Creon (834-1018) is reminiscent of the corresponding scenes between Tiresias and Oedipus in Sophocles' *Oedipus the King* (300-462) and between Tiresias and Creon in *Antigone*, both resulting in a clash (988-1114).[15] The prototype of such confrontation between a king and a prophet is the scene between Agamemnon and Calchas in *Iliad* 1 (68-20). By contrast, in the scene between Creon and Tiresias, Euripides reduces the fierce temper of both characters as Creon too does not even defy the prophet; he accepts the prophecy as valid and only tries to find a way to escape it. In this scene Euripides evokes for his audience their familiarity with the Sophoclean subtexts but also causes surprise by transferring the vehemence of this encounter elsewhere: Euripides only alludes to it, as if to declare his intention not to dramatize it. It is the confrontation between Oedipus' sons and Tiresias, firstly referred to by Eteocles (772-3, 'for he will gladly come to converse with you, but I criticized the craft of divination in the past to him, so that he resents me') and repeated by the prophet, whose emphasis on the frequent exchange serves as an elliptical reference to the vehemence which would have been present, had the scene been dramatized (878-9: 'what did I not do, what words did I not speak and so came to enmity with the sons of Oedipus?'). It is at this point that Euripides evokes the familiarity of his audience with the clash between the hero and the prophet in Sophocles' *Oedipus the King* and *Antigone*, and the effect is to suggest the faulty behaviour of the brothers in the past.[16]

In the case of Oedipus Euripides both draws and deviates from tradition. The *Iliad* (23.679-80) mentions that Oedipus was honoured with funeral games in Thebes after his death, where it is implied that he died fighting. If Oedipus fell in battle he could not have been blind in this version. Oedipus' blindness is a standard feature in tragic presentations of Oedipus but is alluded already in the epic *Thebaid*.[17] In tragedy, starting with Aeschylus' *Seven against Thebes* (783-4), Oedipus' blinding is self-inflicted, with the exception of Euripides' *Oedipus*, where

32

he is blinded by the servants of Laius, probably at Creon's command.[18] The reference to Oedipus' self-blinding in the prologue of the *Phoenician Women* (61-2) is made in a way which recalls the narration of the same event by the Messenger in *Oedipus the King* (1268-70). The key-phrase is the 'golden pins' which Jocasta says that Oedipus used to strike his eyes. In the passage from *Oedipus the King* these are specifically the 'golden pins' of Jocasta's garment that Oedipus tore from his dead wife's dress and used to blind himself. Although the phrasing may be formulaic, and the brooches may be a convenient means for this kind of self-mutilation,[19] Jocasta's use of it in the prologue may have conveyed to an informed audience the sense of a tribute to the Sophoclean passage together with a self-conscious innovation.

In Homer (*Il.* 23.679-80) and Hesiod (fr. 192 M-W) Oedipus is buried at Thebes, while Sophocles varies in his treatment: in *Antigone* (50) Oedipus is said to die in dishonour, and it is implied that he died in Thebes (49-54, 900-3), in *Oedipus the King* his despair makes him wish for solitary wandering (1410-11, 1436-7, 1449-50, 1518) but the end of the play does not specify his condition, and finally in *Oedipus at Colonus* he is exiled, following the city's decision which has been influenced by his sons, and dies at Athens where he becomes a local hero.

The theme of Oedipus' exile is not attested in epic but is known to Pindar (*Pythian Ode* 4. 263). It appears as Oedipus' wish in *Oedipus the King* (1436) and has a central role in the *Phoenician Women*, although it is dramatized in a different dramatic context. Euripides still uses the theme of Oedipus' exile but (as in the case of Jocasta's suicide) postpones it to the end of his drama. In this version Euripides makes Oedipus' exile follow the death of his sons, while in all other extant versions Oedipus is exiled before his sons' mutual killing. Oedipus continues to live in the palace after the revelation of his incest, as the audience hear early in the prologue (66), which may have come as a surprise, if contrasted with other tragic versions. But in epic versions, including Homer and the *Oedipodia*, he continued to be king. On the other hand, Oedipus' loss of power, which is standardized in later versions, is already alluded in the epic *Thebaid*, where his treatment by his sons invokes his curse.[20]

The prologue of the *Phoenician Women* mentions that the two brothers, when they became of age, out of shame confined Oedipus behind closed doors (63-5). It is only after the killing of his sons that Oedipus is brought out of the palace at the call of Antigone (1539ff.). The idea of Oedipus' confinement in the palace is also suggested in Sophocles' *Oedipus the King*, when Creon urges his attendants to take him into the palace so that his pollution is no longer exposed (1423-9). In the *Thebaid* Oedipus is blind and dependent on his sons, whose conduct prompts him to curse them, but it is not certain whether he was imprisoned by them. Euripides' version follows the *Thebaid*, and makes the sons' detention of their father and overall conduct be the dishonour which causes Oedipus to curse them. Oedipus comes to regret his curse. The implied interval between Oedipus' blinding and his detention by his sons may suggest to the audience either that Creon took over the throne[21] or that Oedipus continued to be the king of Thebes after his blinding.[22] In the latter case, the audience may have thought that Euripides uses a variation of the epic version according to which Oedipus, not blind, continued to rule over Thebes.

The strife of Eteocles and Polynices, which results in mutual fratricide, is traditionally associated with Oedipus' curse on his sons, which is variously portrayed as invoked by his sons' actions, sometimes attributed to trivial motivation, or directed against the sons as the embodiment of Oedipus' incest. In *Phoenician Women*, the curse is already mentioned in the prologue (67-8) and refers to the brothers' division of the inheritance by the sword. There is no mention here of the reason that prompted Oedipus' curse on his sons but Tiresias later says that they granted neither prerogatives nor leave to depart to their father and that Oedipus was dishonoured by them (874-7). The mention of the 'denied prerogatives' may refer to the best parts of a sacrificial animal, in which case Euripides may be alluding to the *Thebaid* and Oedipus' anger at his sons when he was not granted the choicest portion of meat.

34

It is after commenting on the sons' failure to send the best part of meat to their father that the scholium on Sophocles' *Oedipus at Colonus* 1375 notes that Aeschylus says something similar in his *Seven against Thebes*. The relevant passage in the Aeschylean play (785-90) has been variously explained.[23] The Chorus attribute Oedipus' curse to his anger at his sons' *tropha* (786), from the verb *trephô*, which may mean food, tending, upbringing or origin.[24] Accordingly, the line in Aeschylus has often been taken as a reference to the meat-portion mentioned in the *Thebaid*, or to a general ill-treatment of Oedipus by his sons. If it referred to the polluted origin of the sons, one may wonder why the curse did not include the two daughters as well, as they were also the offspring of an incestuous union. The brothers may have begun quarrelling after Oedipus' fall and the curse may have been modelled on the circumstances of their dispute. On the other hand, if the word refers to the (incestuous) begetting of the sons, the curse may have been uttered immediately after Oedipus' self-blinding. The content of the curse, as the Chorus say in the passage, is division of the inheritance by the two brothers 'with iron-wielding hand'. The division of the inheritance by the sword and the ensuing bitter reconciliation are important issues in the play (720ff., 816f., 883f.) and it has been argued that they were both mentioned as the content of Oedipus' curse in Aeschylus' *Oedipus*.[25]

In Stesichorus' version the curse does not seem to have played any part, as their mother is made to know her sons' fate only through Tiresias' prophecy. The quarrel of the brothers is central, and Tiresias associates the quarrel with troubles for the family (217, 228, 230-1), but there is no mention of Oedipus' involvement. In the epic *Thebaid*, there seem to have been two curses, one when Polynices defied Oedipus' prohibition and presented to him the table and cup of Laius, and another when both sons failed to send to their father the best portion of meat. In both cases the effect is the same, namely continuous strife over the inheritance and mutual killing. Sophocles (*Oedipus at Colonus* 421ff., 1375ff.) makes Oedipus curse his sons onstage after they have quarrelled. His sons did nothing to help him when Creon decided to drive him away from Thebes and he himself desired to stay. His sons quarrelled over the throne without Oedipus having any involvement in this quarrel, with the effect that Eteocles managed to prevail and expelled Polynices, who in turn came to Oedipus for his blessing, only to receive his curse.

All attempts at solving the strife fail in all versions. In Stesichorus their mother suggests that one should become the king and the other should inherit the possessions and leave Thebes. This is to be decided by lot and both brothers seem to agree. Close to this version is Hellanicus, who reports that Eteocles suggested that Polynices should either rule Thebes or take part of the inheritance and leave the city. In this case the issue was not decided by lot, but Polynices accepted his brother's offer, left the kingdom to Eteocles, took the chiton and necklace of Harmonia and went to Argos, where he presented these gifts to Argia, the king Adrastus' daughter (4F98 *FGrH*). We do not know how Stesichorus and Hellanicus motivated the eventual confrontation. The distinctive feature of their accounts is that there was an original bargain, whereas in other versions Polynices is driven away by force: A Homeric scholium (on *Iliad* 4.376) records that Eteocles as the older[26] brother expelled Polynices, and Pherecydes (3F96 *FGrH*) reports the same version.

In Aeschylus' *Seven against Thebes* the background of the brothers' conflict is not entirely clear. There is the implication that Eteocles expelled his brother (*Seven against Thebes* 637-8) as Polynices is called an 'exiler'. This is reported in the words of the Messenger, who conveys Polynices' perspective and claims. Polynices is similarly reported to make a strong claim that Justice is on his side (642-8). On the other hand, Eteocles strongly denies the justice of his brother's cause (662-71), and he himself is from the very beginning of the drama the central figure as the defender of his city. Rather than commenting on the reasons leading to the current situation, the play stresses the theme of the common fate of the two brothers, which is inextricably linked to their father's curse on them. Although there is an awareness of the dire curse there is also a hope that it can be averted. It is only when Eteocles learns that Polynices will be at the seventh gate that he accepts the inevitable and aligns his will to his father's curse that his sons should divide the inheritance by the sword (785-90). This curse was probably reported in the second play of Aeschylus' Theban tetralogy (*Laius, Oedipus, Seven against Thebes* and the satyric *Sphinx*). When Eteocles comes to realize that his father's curse cannot be averted, he also refers to an earlier dream which foretold the division of the property and has now come true (*Seven against Thebes* 709-11). The content of this dream is not recorded but may have been mentioned in the preceding play. It has been suggested,[27] based on the Chorus' reference that the stranger Chalyb, i.e. steel, is the divider of their inheritance (*Seven against Thebes* 727-33), that the dream in *Oedipus* may have referred to a foreign arbiter coming to divide the patrimony. It is possible that the two brothers came to an agreement which gave hope that the curse would be avoided. If this occurred in *Oedipus*, there would be strong dramatic irony when in the *Seven against Thebes* Eteocles comes to realize that hope was futile, the curse was inescapable and the 'mediator' who would divide the property was steel.

In Sophocles' *Oedipus at Colonus* (367-73) Ismene reports that the brothers originally agreed to leave the throne to Creon but later were overcome by an evil rivalry to grasp royal power. In the *Phoenician Women* Euripides innovates: the two brothers are said to have agreed to rule in alternate years with Polynices voluntarily leaving Thebes for the first year (72, 433-4, 476, 630). This version becomes the most familiar, and later authors such as Diodorus of Sicily (4.65.1) and Apollodorus (*Library* 6.1) follow it, while Hyginus (*Fabula* 67) has Oedipus himself order the alternation of kingship. Euripides' innovation seems to be a modification of the motif of the bargain between the two brothers found in Hellanicus (4F98). He also employs the motif of Polynices' exile by Eteocles, found in Pherecydes (3F96). The scholium on Euripides' *Phoenician Women* 71 notes that Euripides is following partly Pherecydes and partly

Hellanicus. Some sort of original agreement which is violated by Eteocles is reflected in Euripides' *Suppliants*, as Polynices is in voluntary exile and has been wronged by Eteocles in terms of money allowances (150-3, 930-1). In Sophocles' *Antigone* Creon blames Polynices for attacking Thebes (198-202, 280-9, 514-20), while the Chorus refer (111) to the 'contentious disputes' of Polynices in a way which on the one hand seems to put the blame on both brothers but on the other suggestively stresses the responsibility of Polynices by making an etymological play on his name.[28] This name-play is reminiscent of Eteocles' remark in Aeschylus' *Seven against Thebes* (658) that Polynices is very fitly named.

Both Eteocles and Polynices are familiar figures from other tragedies. The difference in the Euripidean portrayal is that Polynices is presented in a more sympathetic light both by comparison with other sources and in relation to Eteocles. In the *Seven against Thebes* Eteocles remains at the centre of the drama throughout as the defender of the city, whereas Polynices, who is presented as the attacker of his city, does not appear onstage. Conversely, Euripides brings Polynices onstage to defend himself. In emphasizing the justice of Polynices, Euripides seems to respond to Aeschylus' *Seven against Thebes*, where Justice was the emblem on Polynices' shield (646-8). Euripides' innovation is sharp, especially when compared to versions where Polynices agrees to take part of the possessions and leave Thebes but later violates the agreement and attacks his city. What informs the background of the Euripidean portrayal of both brothers is their awareness of their father's curse and their eager wish to avoid its dire consequence, mutual fratricide, by choosing to stay physically apart from each other. This is a conscious attempt, found also in Stesichorus and Hellanicus (and possibly Aeschylus).[29]

Although several of the warriors involved in the expedition against Thebes are known from earlier tradition, Aeschylus' *Seven against Thebes* is the first known source to present seven warriors at seven gates. Euripides' *Phoenician Women* gives a different version of the fighting between the combatants, which contains none of the Aeschylean symmetry of the seven duels at the seven gates. After both Capaneus' and Parthenopaeus' deaths, Adrastus decides to withdraw his army (1141-99, 1219-39). Eteocles then suggests that the outcome should be decided by a duel between himself and his brother Polynices. In the single combat (1356ff.) he manages to inflict a fatal wound on Polynices but when he fails to kill him and take the spoils, his brother strikes him too and both brothers die. Their death at each other's hand is followed by Jocasta' suicide over the corpses of her sons (1455-9). There is an obvious allusion to the Aeschylean description of the seven pairs of fighters in the *Seven against Thebes*, which Euripides pointedly refuses to elaborate (751). By saying that it would be a waste of time to state the name of each of the seven defenders at the gates, the Euripidean Eteocles erases the central part of the Aeschylean play, where the names and attributes of these fighters were reported in detail. The reason given by Eteocles in Euripides, namely, that there should be no delay in action (753), may be viewed as a wish to substitute dramatic action for the static description which characterizes the Aeschylean play.[30]

An essential novelty compared to the Aeschylean account is structural. In Aeschylus, the main part of the drama consisted in the seven pairs of speeches between the Theban Scout and Eteocles, where the Scout described the attacker at each gate, laying great emphasis on the emblem of each shield, and Eteocles responded by announcing an appropriate defender. The climactic exchange culminated in the announcement of Polynices at the seventh gate and Eteocles' decision to confront his own brother. The result of the encounter, that is, salvation for the city but mutual fratricide for Eteocles and Polynices, was later announced by the Messenger. This tight Aeschylean architectural structure is abandoned by Euripides in favour of a technique which multiplies the accounts and the perspectives. Euripides uses a manifold perspective. In the Teichoskopia scene (88-201),[31] where the first perspective on the invading army is given, Antigone asks about the identity of the attackers she sees from the wall and the Tutor identifies each one in turn.

Whereas in Aeschylus the emblems on the shields of the attackers had a symbolic function, Euripides makes them a means for recognizing the identity of each warrior. Whereas the Aeschylean Scout stressed the arrogance of the attackers, the Euripidean Tutor, although he of course wishes the Thebans to prevail, expresses the view that the attackers come to Thebes with justice (154). This important remark is an early sign of Euripides' deviation from Aeschylus in presenting a more favourable portrayal of Polynices in his drama.

The Aeschylean atmosphere of imminent danger, which caused the panic of the female Chorus,[32] is here transformed. Although the Argive army is said to be on the move, there is enough time for the dialogue between the Tutor and Antigone, and although Antigone is of course presented as concerned, her anxiety remains controlled. In substituting Antigone's reaction to the Argive attack for that of the Aeschylean Chorus, Euripides achieves two dramatic purposes: he gives a more detached part to his Chorus[33] and also minimizes the extent of the external threat as Antigone, a young girl, shows greater composure than the women of the Aeschylean Chorus.

The Tutor's remark on the justice of the attackers, along with Antigone's longing to rush and throw her arms around her 'piteous exile' brother (167) are clear hints that Euripides' play will offer a different dramatization of the conflict between the two brothers. At the same time, the Tutor's encouragement to Antigone to be confident for 'internally at least the city is secure' (117) is a remark which may be said to allude to the Aeschylean Eteocles, who was presented as the confident leader whose decisions were meant to secure the safety of his city. By contrast, Euripides problematizes the role of Eteocles and deprives him of any claim to be a good ruler. The Tutor's remark is ironic when read against the development of the plot. He means of course that the city inside is safe because it is free. But the city internally turns out to be the problem, as it is Eteocles' attitude as leader and his violation of Polynices' rights that have caused the external attack. The Teichoskopia scene proves to be the first stage in Euripides' rewriting of the central scene of Aeschylus' play. Whereas Aeschylus relied on the Scout's reports and Eteocles' 'reading' of the symbolism of the enemy-emblems, Euripides dramatizes a scene based almost entirely on the gaze.[34] Antigone and the Tutor both look from the top of the walls at the enemy outside. Their gaze also directs the audience's attention from the inside to the outside. But the gaze is not accompanied by interpretation, as the audience are not given any symbolic reading of the enemy weapons, but is restricted to the function of identification, hence is kept on a superficial level. In this respect, the direction of the attention both of the characters and of the audience outwards is implied to be a diversion from the central problem which lies within.

The second perspective on the Argive attack is that in the scene between Eteocles and Creon in the second episode. The decision to station one commander at each of the seven gates is no longer an idea of Eteocles but a suggestion put forward by Creon (741). The emphasis is not, as in Aeschylus, on the duels between the warriors. In answer to Eteocles' question whether these seven defenders are to be commanders of detachments or prepare for single combat Creon suggests detachments (743). This shifts the emphasis from the individual to the general battle. Creon's opinion that a single man cannot see everything (745), which sounds like a maxim, may perhaps function as a comment on a shift in this play from the Aeschylean emphasis on the confrontation between individuals towards a preference for showing the enemy more as a collective body. In this context, Eteocles' reluctance to state the name of each defender (751) may be taken as a hint of this new perception of the attackers as a whole, where there is no climactic process leading to the fight between the two brothers as in Aeschylus.

The third and fourth perspectives on the Argive army are given in the account of the Messenger, who describes first the emblems of the seven commanders of the enemy (1104-40) and then the ensuing battle between the two armies (1141-99). The section on the emblems is the closer one to the Aeschylean play but again the individuality of the commanders is clearly not the focus of the Euripidean treatment. It is telling that the

Messenger makes references to the armies as collective bodies soon to join battle (1096-1103), while the part of the account devoted to the actual fight is clearly a description of armies in battle. Again Euripides undermines the Aeschylean atmosphere of imminent threat as the entire description of the enemies and their impending attack is narrated at a time when the battle is over and the outcome is victorious for the Thebans. The Messenger reports the good news to Jocasta (1079), hence the entire account is made against a background of relief and not, as in Aeschylus, of anxiety. Therefore, the emblems are not the type of symbols interpreted as self-ominous by Eteocles before the battle but are simply described by the Messenger in a way which makes their symbolism, if any, open to interpretation on the basis of the already stated defeat of their owners.

The Argive emblems are presented as less arrogant compared to their Aeschylean precedents, perhaps because Euripides stresses the justice of Polynices' cause. Overall, the Euripidean passage (1104-40)[35] is much shorter and has a peripheral function compared to the lengthy Aeschylean descriptions of the Argive shields, which lie at the core of the *Seven against Thebes*. The Euripidean shield scene is also delayed until after, and not before, the first battle and the defeat of the Argives and thus plays down the atmosphere of imminent threat which permeates the Aeschylean play. This removes the inconsistency which might arise in relation to the stated implication that there would be no detailed description of the warriors (751). There is nothing to match the interpretation of the semiotics of the shields and the corresponding allocation of champions by the Aeschylean Eteocles. Whether this is to be viewed as a deliberate deconstruction of the Aeschylean symbolism of the shields or as a new set of symbols where the audience and not Eteocles is given the role of the interpreter,[36] Euripides dissociates the fight of the brothers from the other duels. A telling novelty is that Eteocles is not stationed at a specific gate, hence there is no climactic process leading up to the fight between himself and Polynices, and the decision that the two brothers fight each other is made by Eteocles himself at a time when the Thebans are victorious.

The perspective on the Argive invading army is supplemented by the detailed account of the duel between Eteocles and Polynices (1356-424). Euripides follows Homeric duel-narratives which are often the focus within a context of large-scale encounters between opposing forces. The reminiscence of a Homeric combat can be seen as offering a sense of epic grandeur to the two duellists. At the same time, however, this is undermined in a typically Euripidean manner (see Chapter 1), when both combatants fail to achieve epic status. Although the narrative is rich in epic elements, including the prayers of the combatants, the presence of onlookers or the mode of fighting, the overall Euripidean emphasis on realistic presentation, including a reference to a wrestling trick (1407-13)[37], evokes athletic tactics familiar to the fifth-century audience, thus stripping the duellists from a sense of distant grandeur.[38]

The prototype, in particular, of a duel which is decided in order to prevent bloodshed on both opposing armies is that between Menelaus and Paris in *Iliad* 3 (84-115, 324-80).[39] In the Homeric passage (66-75, 86-102) Paris suggests that there should be a single combat between himself and Menelaus so that there should be no more bloodshed between the Trojans and the Greeks, and Menelaus agrees. Similarly in Euripides Eteocles suggests that he should fight a duel with his brother so that no more Thebans and Argives die in battle, and Polynices agrees (1225-37). According to Mastronarde,[40] Euripides' adaptation of the Homeric model has two distinctive features. Firstly, the solution of the single combat to forestall further deaths, placed as it is after, and not before, the first battle which has already cost numerous deaths on both sides, reduces the heroic element of this decision. On this view, there is no such irony in the Iliadic passage, for there, the duel between Paris and Menelaus is presented, in narrative terms, at the beginning of the war. Secondly, the outcome of the duel causes the opposite of the intended result, as both the Thebans and the Argives claim victory for themselves and rush to arms causing further bloodshed (1460-71).

However, it seems that in both cases Euripides is rather following the ironic context within which the duel is presented by Homer. More broadly, it seems that the end of the second and the third book of the *Iliad* have functioned as the subtext of the Euripidean play on a wider scale than has already been noticed, as in both cases a city (Troy, Thebes) is at the moment of being attacked by an army (Greeks, Argives); the invading leaders are presented in a catalogue; a leader (Hector, Eteocles) organizes the defence; and a duel is decided to settle the issue (Paris–Menelaus, Eteocles–Polynices). Euripides makes use of the alleged justice of the Greek attack, as in Homer Menelaus and the Greeks claim that they want recompense for the abduction of Helen by Paris. Similarly, one of the novelties that Euripides introduces is that Polynices pleads his case on the basis of the violation of his rights that he has suffered by Eteocles. The *Iliad*, with its complex sympathy for both Greeks and Trojans, turns out to be a more appropriate model for the Euripidean dramatization of the Argive attack against Thebes, than the *Thebaid*, which seems to have portrayed the attackers (with the exception of Amphiaraus) as embodiments of arrogance in the way that Aeschylus portrayed them in his *Seven against Thebes*, the tragedy closest in time to the *Thebaid*.[41]

In *Iliad* 3 Priam mentions that Menelaus, along with Odysseus, had been to Troy before because of Helen (206). This information, also mentioned in *Iliad* 11 (138-42), refers to Menelaus' peaceful mission to Troy where he requested the return of Helen. It was the failure of this mission that led to the expedition against Troy. At a certain point in Euripides' *Phoenician Women*, a scholium seems to perceive a wider intertextual relation with Book 3. When in the Teichoskopia scene Antigone expresses her longing to see Polynices, the Tutor tells her that her brother 'will come to these halls so as to fill you with joy, under truce' (170-1). The scholium on l. 170 remarks that in making Polynices come to Thebes under truce Euripides is imitating the Homeric Menelaus, who went to Troy in order

44

to put off war. By contrast, it is this underlying parallelism between Polynices and the Homeric Menelaus that another ancient scholiast misses when he remarks, in a note preserved as the third ancient preface to the play, that 'Polynices comes under truce for no reason'. At this point in the Teichoskopia scene Euripides builds expectation and suspense on the part of Antigone and the audience, while the actual development of the plot brings Polynices onstage, as Menelaus went to Troy, but the outcome, as in the case of Menelaus, was fruitless. At the same time, Euripides lays the foundation for dramatic irony in building this anticipation for a happy reunion, as Antigone will see her brother only when he is dying.

The fact that the Homeric Paris' decision to engage in single combat with Menelaus follows his cowardice at the sight of Menelaus in the battlefield and his rebuke from Hector (*Iliad* 3.30-57) undermines his seemingly heroic offer designed to spare the lives of the Trojan and Greek troops. In Euripides the suggestion of the duel between the protagonists of the dispute comes after a first engagement between the two armies as in Homer the duel between Menelaus and Paris follows the preparations for a battle between the troops. The main point of comparison is not so much the difference in dramatic terms, that is, that the audience are invited to think that in Euripides Eteocles' suggestion comes too late, as there have already been victims, whereas in Homer Paris' similar offer is well-timed. Rather, the audience are invited to think that in both cases the suggestion of the duel comes from the person who originally caused the dispute by violating the other's rights, that is, Eteocles with regard to depriving his brothers of his rights to the throne and Paris with regard to taking Menelaus' wife and refusing to return her. Therefore, Euripides is exploiting the irony which is already present in the Homeric account, as in both cases selfishness negates the admission of fault and the use of good sense and leads to the use of violence, which proves unable to resolve the impasse. So, in both cases the result of the duel, Paris' prompt salvation by Aphrodite's intervention in Homer and mutual fratricide in Euripides, leads to a full-scale engagement of the troops as the War at Troy continues and the Thebans and Argives join in battle. Because Eteocles' suggestion of a duel is based on his selfish reluctance to admit he has been wrong, even his claim that his intention is to prevent further bloodshed in his city is ironically undermined and proven to be empty rhetoric. In this respect, the audience are invited to think that a real concern for the city would make Eteocles recognize his guilt. Instead of this, Eteocles resembles the Homeric Paris, who both before and after his duel with Menelaus did not admit his responsibility.

Homer's emphasis on Helen's perspective in both book 3 and book 6 of the *Iliad* and on her regret serves to emphasize further Paris' egoism. It is telling that in book 6 (328-9) Hector rebukes Paris again for the plight suffered by the Trojans on his behalf in a way which mirrors the similar situation which led to the duel depicted in book 3, and reveals that Paris' self-centred attitude has not changed since then. Already at the end of book 3, the erotic desire felt by Paris for Helen (441-8), seemingly ill-timed, as it follows the duel and Helen's rebukes, is in fact an opportune means of evoking and repeating the original abduction of Helen by Paris, thus stressing Paris' selfish complacence with his past actions. It is just such an egoistical refusal to admit one's wrong that is characteristic also of the Euripidean Eteocles. This egoism is highlighted by the stress on Polynices' justice, but Euripides reserves a sharper contrast for another action. After all, Polynices may have been wronged by his brother in the past and may have been consequently given a just grievance, yet he did not hesitate to attack his own homeland and cause the deaths of Thebans. Hence, neither of the brothers shows true, that is, unselfish concern for his city. The violence of the fratricide resolves the dispute between the two brothers, where however the interest of the city is subordinated by each one's concern for power. This is contrasted by Euripides with the violence of the sacrifice of Menoeceus, whose action proves to be an unselfish self-sacrifice for the safety of the city.

Finally, the modelling of the Teichoskopia scene in the *Phoenician Women* on the famous Homeric Teichoskopia in

Iliad 3 (161-244) was already noted by a scholiast on Euripides' *Phoenician Women* 88, who also remarks the reversal of the roles of the interlocutor and the informant, as in Homer it is a woman (Helen) who shows the warriors to an old man (Priam), whereas in the drama it is an old man (the Tutor) who shows the champions to a girl (Antigone). In Homer the scene, which follows the announcement of the impending duel between Paris and Menelaus (121-60), is an exchange between Priam and Helen which takes place at a time of war but not of imminent danger, as the Trojan and Greek armies are both seated and wait for what they believe to be the event (i.e. the duel) which will halt war. In Euripides the scene takes place soon before the attack of the Argive army, but at a time when dialogue is still possible, while the event (i.e. the duel) which will allegedly put an end to the war is postponed to a later part of the dramatic action.

The positive description of the Greek leaders in Homer is an element that has found its way into the Euripidean narrative: although the invading army is an enemy, there is nothing like its Aeschylean counterpart when the Tutor is made to remark that it has justice on its side (154). The information of Helen, guided by Priam's questions, gives long accounts on Agamemnon and Odysseus, and shorter accounts on Ajax and Idomeneus. After that Helen ends her account, saying that she sees all the Argive leaders and that she could identify them all but her concern is the whereabouts of her two brothers, the Dioscuri. It is here that the scene ends, followed by the Homeric narrator's remark that Helen's brothers have died (243-4). It has rightly been pointed out that Helen's concern for her two brothers, whom she cannot see in the plain, may have suggested to Euripides the idea of a similar scene in which his Antigone expresses her love for her brother and the difficulty in discerning him in the distance.[42] Another intertextual relation that may have suggested itself to Euripides is the *aposiopesis* (suppression of mention) used by Helen. In Homer, this *aposiopesis* is an apt way of avoiding the monotony that might have arisen from a long identification-exposition of the Greek heroes, especially if one thinks that such a long catalogue formed a great part of book 2. A similar *aposiopesis* is used not here but in the scene where the Euripidean Eteocles opts not to give a full list of the names of the warriors at each gate (751) and may have been suggested to Euripides by the Homeric scene, which, as a whole, forms a subtext of his play.

Overall, Euripides's treatment of the myth reveals a wide knowledge of earlier versions and a strong self-consciousness about its relation to tradition. The appearance of Jocasta and Oedipus is meant to surprise the audience, and bringing Polynices onstage to argue his case is an attempt to dramatize the brothers' dispute from a balanced perspective. But Euripides does not take sides and his intertextual allusions to a number of passages imply the complex nature of the motives behind the brother's clash. The introduction of the character of Menoeceus and his self-sacrifice is presented as an alternative to the brothers' self-interested motives and invites the audience to think about the central theme of the juxtaposition between the civic and the individualistic interest.

3

Characters and Actions

Greek tragedians set the plot-line and the series of actions and then elaborate the characters who bring these actions into completion. But the priority of action (cf. Aristotle's *Poetics* chapter 6) does not mean that a character's consistency can be sacrificed to the requirements of a dramatic plot. The dramatists treat their characters as integral parts in the connected series of the dramatic events. Characters express their motivation through the medium of their words and become agents through their interaction with external factors. Euripides' *Phoenician Women* is exceptionally rich in terms of both character and event (see Chapter 1). This chapter will examine the relation between characterization and action as a means of illuminating central dramatic concerns. Jocasta, who opens the drama, as well as Polynices and Eteocles, whose strife is the main theme of the drama, will be the first characters to be discussed, followed by an examination of all other characters in turn.

Jocasta

Although sometimes criticized as an unjustifiably long exposition of detail,[1] Jocasta's opening monologue (1-87) has a strong dramatic effect, as it includes Euripidean innovations to the myth (see Chapter 2) and arouses interest as to what is to follow. Jocasta's reflection on the past shows her deep awareness of the pattern of repetition in the House of the Labdacids, that is, of the plight and unhappiness that strike each generation in turn, starting from Laius, then affecting

Oedipus and now Oedipus' sons. Her calm exposition suggests a character whose painful experience has made her able to reflect that human plight is the result of both human faults and inexorable fate.

Jocasta dissociates herself from past crimes, as these are attributed to Laius' transgression and Jocasta implies that she had no involvement. This is quite different to the Sophoclean Jocasta (in *Oedipus the King*) who seemed to have collaborated with Laius in the past, and in her exchange with Oedipus tried to dissuade him from pursuing the truth. She is also different from the mother in Stesichorus' version (see Chapter 2), since she now clearly states that the decision to take turns in ruling, which proved disastrous, was the idea of her sons (69-74). It is only at the end of the monologue, with the use of the first person 'I persuaded' (81-2) that the Euripidean Jocasta marks a break from her passivity in the past and announces the active role she is about to play.[2] The active part implies that she, a woman, has undertaken a role typically reserved for men. Her initiative to invite Polynices to come uses the technical term *hypospondos* ('under truce', 81), which refers to an agreement proposed by a political or military leader.[3] But although this portrayal of Jocasta as the central figure who cares for the city may be said to approximate her to leaders such as Eteocles at the beginning of Aeschylus' *Seven against Thebes* or Oedipus at the beginning of *Oedipus the King*,[4] she never ceases to have the typical female and maternal role of being primarily concerned with the safety of her family.[5]

Her relation to Oedipus is that of understanding and sympathy as she stresses both his innocence and the immensity of his sufferings (53, 60). She is presented as standing by Oedipus, and her loyalty and compassion are evoked after her death by Oedipus towards the end of the play, where (1617) he expresses his certainty that Jocasta would support him and accompany him to exile if alive.[6]

Her outline of the strife is a balanced exposition of the brothers' claims, which prepares for their argumentations in the *agôn*. Eteocles is clearly said to have been the one to violate the pact, thus starting the strife, while Polynices' demand of his share has made him bring a foreign army against his homeland (71-80). The mention of Eteocles' violation of the deal may be taken as a hint at the Euripidean innovation in giving a more favourable portrayal of Polynices compared to other versions. Euripides may have even given an earlier hint, when Jocasta first refers to her sons as 'Eteocles and glorious (*kleinên*) in might Polynices' (56). The epic periphrasis dignifies Polynices but also introduces a verbal pun where the epithet *kleinos* 'glorious' used for Polynices recalls the name Eteocles ('true-glory') and would thus be more appropriate to him.[7] It is as if for a moment Polynices is given the glory of his brother or, in other words, as if Euripides is suggesting to his audience that his Polynices will be different. This phrasing however should not be taken as an indication of Jocasta's preference for Polynices but understood rather as due to Polynices' long absence away from his mother.[8] One can read, however, a further connotation in this approximation of Polynices and Eteocles in phrasing: it may be an allusion to their similarities which lead to their refusal to yield and undermine any attempt at reconciliation as will become evident in the *agôn* scene.

Jocasta's initiative gives her an active part in a crisis which is both familial and political. She is one of the Euripidean women of authority, like Aethra in *Suppliants*, who have the wisdom and the determination to take action and bring a solution to the crisis.[9] She puts her trust on the gods, though her reference to Zeus's remote seat in the heavens (84) ironically suggests the gap between gods and humans. During her emotional outburst in the scene with Polynices she clearly calls Eteocles' exiling of Polynices 'an outrage' (319), while in both the prologue and later she avoids taking sides and tries to remain neutral. She embraces her son and steps around him in the form of a dance (316), which for the aged Jocasta who drags her tread (302-3) may be taken as an indication that the joy she experiences has almost rejuvenated her.[10] Her monody is a conglomerate of joy and sorrow as the absence of Polynices is likened to death: Shearing off her hair, refusing any joy and wearing gloomy rags (322-5) is a process of an endless grief which amounts to mourning of the dead, reminiscent to a certain degree of Electra's mourning of her brother Orestes in Sophocles.[11] Apart from the function of mourning of her exiled son whom she may have feared to be dead (cf. scholium on 323), her black costume has the dramaturgical effect of ominous anticipation; that is, it functions as a visual hint for the audience of the eventual death of Jocasta's sons (see Chapter 5).

Her moral that 'one must endure what the gods send' (382), which will be recalled at the end of the play in Oedipus' remark that 'for being mortal one must endure compulsion sent by the gods' (1763), is an implicit equation of the human condition with suffering.[12] It is, however, an indication of neither resignation[13] nor pessimism[14] but rather a conscious plea for action based on human limitations. The exchange between mother and son introduces the theme of exile (388ff.), which is a recurrent topic[15] in the play, and Jocasta thus finds the opportunity to explore with her son the theme of love for one's country. This invites the audience to start thinking about what was hinted at the prologue: Polynices was wronged in being exiled, but does his longing to return to his homeland turn out to be not an unselfish love, when he is determined to sack it in order to achieve his goal?

In the *agôn* scene of the second episode (443-637)[16] Jocasta has the role of the arbitrator between Polynices (the plaintiff) and Eteocles (the defendant), who argue for their cases in turn. This is a typical pattern in *agônes*, the formal debates which had a strong appeal to the Athenians with their passion for lawcourts, but a difference is that Jocasta has no power to decide the outcome and give a verdict. Her role is to try to achieve reconciliation, but what the debate reveals is the strong juxtaposition between the two brothers' worldviews.[17] As Mastronarde[18] has argued, Jocasta is one of Euripides' 'optimistic rationalists' (like Theseus in the *Suppliants* or Tiresias in the *Bacchae*), that is, a figure who combines traditional values and intellectual modernity and believes that the world is orderly, intelligible and designed for the good of humanity.

Human beings in turn are meant to use and uphold this harmony which is sent by the gods. This optimistic rationalism may be appealing to the audience, but the course of the plays standardly renders it futile. In the case of Jocasta, it reveals her as a tragic person, as her intervention not only falls on deaf ears but leads to the most abrupt escalation of the verbal confrontation between the brothers, ending with their wish to fight each other in battle (621-4).

Although Jocasta's criticism of ambition for power and tyranny (which she regards as synonyms[19]) is traditional, it may have conveyed to the audience contemporary political connotations, given that the word *philotimia* was used disparagingly in the period around 411 BC (oligarchic regime), when the Athenians were torn between the partisans of oligarchy and the democrats.[20] The topicality of the idea of reconciliation at the end of the fifth century is reinforced by its importance in Aristophanes' *Lysistrata* and *Frogs*.[21] It has indeed been argued[22] that the *agôn* scene in the Euripidean play may be intentionally reminiscent of the reconciliation scene in *Lysistrata*, where Lysistrata successfully intervenes between the Athenian and the Spartan ambassadors. In this case, this would be one example of Euripidean experimentation with the tragic genre and of his technique of 'translating' comic elements into his tragedies in order to heighten serious aspects of his dramas.[23] In our case, the comparison with the successful Lysistrata bitterly stresses that good intentions, wisdom and persuasion are doomed to fail when directed to people who are unwilling to hear anything but their own impulses for possessions and sovereignty; hence the ultimate responsibility lies with Eteocles and Polynices, who both refuse to make concessions as they place their own self-interest above the salvation of their family and fatherland.

Jocasta's argumentation includes several 'modern' ideas that reveal philosophic influence: She is preoccupied with the idea of justice (532, 548, 549), a recurrent motif in the play, but although this and its association with equality are traditional both in their ethical and political dimensions (e.g. Solon

36.18 West), Jocasta associates justice with the order of the universe. She personifies the idea of *isotês* ('equity'), as Eteocles personified and deified the idea of tyranny/monarchy (506), and describes it as a cosmic principle of universal applicability (541-6), which has taken the form of cyclic change, succession of opposites or periodicity,[24] as happens, for example, when day and night succeed each other in turn. The philosopher Heracleitus, who focused on the juxtaposition and unity of opposites, had remarked that 'The Sun shall not outdo the day; otherwise, the Furies, helpers of Justice, shall find him' (fr. 94 D-K).[25] In the Euripidean passage, equality takes on a political resonance which evokes the ideal of the same political and legal rights as the prerequisite of democracy. This ideal informed the political discourse of the Athenians of the fifth century and is reflected for example both in Pericles' discussion of the Athenian democracy in Thucydides (2.37.1) and in Theseus' similar remarks in Euripides' *Suppliants* (404).[26]

Jocasta significantly uses the terms *pleon* 'greater' or 'excess' (540, 553), which sophists like Callicles and Thrasymachus were said to have employed to refer to men's striving to achieve power and property.[27] She argues that equity is in accord to the law (*nomimon*, 538),[28] as the 'lesser' is in constant strife with the 'greater' (538-9). There may be an echo of the dichotomy between law and nature and the sophists' preference for law. But Jocasta seems to imply a universal law about equity, which embraces the entire universe, cosmic and human. She also mentions equity in terms of numbers, weights and measures (541-2) and associates the equity in the social and political realms with the harmony in the sphere of mathematics. In all cases equity involves a standard regularity. An extreme case when equality is destroyed would be beliefs such as those familiar from Plato's picture of Thrasymachus in his *Republic* (book 1.336ff: 'justice is the rule of the strong') and of Callicles in *Gorgias* (482C4ff.: 'that which is right by nature is superior to our laws').[29] Thrasymachus was reported as saying that injustice provides benefits and happiness (Plato's *Republic*

1.344a) and this may be implied in Jocasta's ironic use of the striking oxymoron 'happy injustice' (549).[30]

Jocasta's attempted mediation between her sons will be repeated in the fourth episode (1067-283). The first indication that Euripides gives of this parallelism is in the direct address of the Messenger to Jocasta at the end of his narrative: 'But, if you have some power or wise words or spells to charm, go, restrain your sons from dread conflict. For the danger is extreme' (1259-61). The reference to 'wise words', that is, the use of persuasion, recalls Jocasta's mediation between her sons in the *agôn*,[31] while the reference to spells to charm implies the use of any means that would influence the sons and achieve affectionate reconciliation if rational argument were to fail. This latter prepares for the scene of pathos between Jocasta and her sons, which is reserved for the battlefield, but at a time when it is too late.

Reconciliation is renewed as the target of the dramatic action, mirroring the first part of the play, but now in a heightened sense due to the urgency of the situation. The ensuing action leading to Jocasta's suicide is narrated by the Messenger (1427-59). Jocasta's act of rushing into the battlefield, the domain of men, means a female intrusion into the male world; but this intrusion represents no breach in order, but is meant to imply to the audience the extremity of a mother's love for her children, which does not hesitate to defy boundaries.[32] Her cries of grief and the last words of Polynices, both in quoted speech, as well as the silent tears of Eteocles, are meant to arouse the emotions of the audience, who have the entire scene brought verbally before their eyes. When Jocasta rushed to the battlefield, the Messenger called her 'suffering' or 'wretched' (*talaina*, 1429), whereas now that both her sons die, he uses the much stronger term *huperpathêsasa* (1456 'super-suffering'). The scene culminates in the description of Jocasta seizing a sword from the corpses, stabbing herself to death and falling with her arms round both her sons. The peculiarities of her death signify a gender reversal:[33] death on the battlefield as well as by means of the sword suggests masculinity, whereas self-imposed death as well as driving the sword through the neck (as opposed to the chest) suggest femininity.[34] Both male and female aspects are again combined in the character of Jocasta in the same way that at the beginning of the drama Jocasta behaved both as a mother and as a political leader in absence of a male authoritative figure.

Another perspective used to help the audience reconstruct the off-stage event of Jocasta's death is that of Antigone, the most emotionally involved eyewitness. Antigone's account repeats as well as adds emotive details. A tearful Jocasta is said to have bared her breast to her sons in supplication (1566-9). This has been taken as a discrepancy from the Messenger's report, as it is now implied that Jocasta supplicated her sons before their combat and then witnessed their fight. Mastronarde[35] argues that Euripides tolerates the discrepancy of the two accounts for pathetic effect. However, it may be argued, on the basis of character-perspective, that when Antigone describes Jocasta's holding out her breast in supplication of her sons she describes (in imperfect tense, 1568) Jocasta's intention to use this psychologically strong means of entreaty to her sons (cf. 1278). It is important that when Jocasta urges Antigone to hurry she gives a great emphasis to the need for an opportune arrival (1279-81). This raises audience expectation to the effect that Jocasta's too-late arrival is meant to be the anti-climax which marks the reversal for both her and the audience.

A mother's holding out of her breast to her son in supplication is a traditional *topos* of extreme entreaty in Greek literature, starting from that of Hecuba to Hector in Homer (*Iliad* 22.80). It is, however, an ominous act of supplication as it usually results in failure. In Jocasta's case, what was intended as a supplication becomes a different type of gesture when she falls on her dying sons, embracing and addressing them. This is what the Messenger first described and for the act of 'falling on' he used a participle of the verb *prospitnô* (1433), a verb also employed for supplication proper, as if to convey to the audience the resemblance of Jocasta's gesture to an actual supplication.

As the Messenger reports, Jocasta lamented the great effort of her breasts, that is, the nurture she had offered to her children (1434). This reference here matches both the seeming supplication and the actual maternal supplication that Jocasta intended to carry out.

Antigone then (1570) makes a sharp contrast between Jocasta's intention and what she actually found, that is, as the Messenger earlier described, her sons on the point of death. She found them like lions fighting over a lair lying in blood and dying in what Antigone describes as a cold libation of blood offered by the god Ares to Hades. The mention of the cold (that is, of death) and also the word *êdê* ('already', 1575) suggest that Jocasta finds her sons at a time when they were departing life (cf. 1428) after having fatally wounded each other.[36] Overall, Antigone's account complements the Messenger's report, provides the audience with additional information, exploits the dynamic of the metaphor of supplication and gives a lyric reworking of Jocasta's suicide over her dead sons. Nothing is mentioned of Eteocles' and Polynices' reactions before dying and Antigone closes her account with the mention of Jocasta's suicide and falling amid her sons. In terms of plot-management, this is meant to avoid repetitiousness, while in terms of dramatic effect it may be perceived as a sensitive attempt on the part of Antigone not to linger more on the grievous events that she narrates to her father.

Polynices

Already in the prologue Euripides gives clues to his audience to expect a sympathetic portrayal of Polynices (74-6, 154, 167). His entry in fear, sword in hand and looking around (261-8) at the beginning of the first episode, has been sometimes interpreted as comic (267-9).[37] But his fear is explained by the fact that Polynices is now an enemy of Thebes and faces danger on entering his home-city. His image is comparable to that of Orestes and Pylades when they enter a foreign land in Euripides' *Iphigenia among the Taurians* (67ff.) or to Heracles, when he returns secretly to Thebes fearing danger in Euripides' *Heracles* (595-8). However, this specific portrayal may also hint to the audience that Polynices, though cast in more favourable terms, is still a flawed hero. In this respect, Polynices' fear contrasts with the heroic image of the warrior who stands out in his shining armour, as Antigone had described him (167-9). This image of almost epic grandeur will be repeated in Antigone's words to Oedipus, where she describes the fight between the brothers as one between lions, in a simile and language reminiscent of epic (1573-6). Her brief description there almost summarizes in tone the Messenger's description of the combat (1356-424), which is reminiscent of a Homeric duel and rich in epic colouring.[38] But at the same time the narrative of the duel undermines epic grandeur by means of a realism which brings the heroes to the level of everyday life (see Chapter 2).[39] Euripides thus mingles the heroic with the ordinary in Polynices' image in the course of the play in order to suggest his inadequacy.

A sense of equivocation characterizes Polynices from the beginning (272, 357), where the use of oxymoron, a rhetorical scheme often found in Euripides,[40] here reveals Polynices' uncertainty and fear. This ambivalent state is explained by the paradox that although he enters his beloved country he knows he has come to enemies (358-9). His phrasing, however, raises questions. The maxim that it is inevitable ('by necessity', 358) that all people love their country (358-9) may sound appealing to the audience but in Polynices' case it invites speculation: not all people love their country, or there would be no treason, but most importantly, some people believe that they love their country but at times of crisis place their own personal interest above the general interest of their country. The underlying question is how each person perceives the idea of patriotism and in Polynices' case his words unveil an empty conviction.

His exchange with Jocasta helps to depict a sympathetic Polynices, who shows his affection for his mother as well as his concern for his father and two sisters (376-7, cf. 615, 617, 1445). He stresses that he is the victim of injustice and swears to the gods that it is against his will that he has brought a foreign army (433-4). That he was wronged by Eteocles is a fact that has been corroborated by Jocasta, implied by both the Tutor (154-5) and the Chorus (258-60), and, most importantly, it will be tacitly conceded by Eteocles himself in the *agôn* scene. But Polynices' claim that he has been forced unwillingly to attack his homeland is empty rhetoric: In this sense, the emphasis on the theme of exile (388-407), which arouses sympathy for Polynices' plight in evoking the injustice he has suffered and nostalgia for his country, turns out to highlight his individualistic motives, as this nostalgia degenerates into an ardent wish to acquire political power by means of threatening the safety of the innocent Thebans.

Polynices' mention, in particular, of the exile's lack of freedom of speech, which resembles, according to Jocasta, the status of a slave (391-2) is meant to strike a chord in the Athenian audience, for whom freedom of speech was of paramount importance in their democracy.[41] But he admits that for the sake of getting some advantage during exile one must play the slave against one's nature. The scholium on 395 has condemned this as undignified for a hero. Mastronarde[42] has counterargued that Euripides here shows 'the strain between Polynices' aristocratic beliefs and the situation in which he has found himself'. But the notion is reminiscent of the doctrine 'the end justifies the means' and the word *kerdos* ('profit', 394) may imply not simply sustenance but any advantage. The idea also implies that one's nature, which in Polynices' case refers to his nobility, can be deformed by misfortune. This idea will be stressed when Polynices insists that his lineage did not feed him when he was reduced to a state of poverty (405), and also closes his speech when he says that he has decided the expedition against Thebes because a poor man cannot be noble (441-2). The emphasis on wealth *versus* poverty, which seems to imply that Polynices' motive is greed, has led several critics, who argued for the favourable characterization of Polynices throughout, to delete verses 438-42.[43] Mastronarde[44] has convincingly argued instead that Polynices' concern with property is conventional and reflects the aristocratic value-system, where nobility and wealth are combined.

The question of whether nobility is fixed or vulnerable in the face of adversity is a familiar topic in Euripides, which relates to the debate on the value of *phusis* (nature) *versus nomos* (referring to nurture), a debate current in the fifth century and given further impetus by the sophists, who favoured the importance of *nomos*. Polynices, although presented as following traditional aristocratic values, implies the non-traditional notion that nature is inferior to *nomos*. At the same time his view that nobility is negated by adversity contrasts with the view that nobility does not perish in misfortune (voiced in the same play by Oedipus, 1623-4). Overall, his course of thinking seems to be governed by his wish to find arguments in favour of his expedition against his city and rationalize it for himself, the other characters and the audience. This is not to say that Polynices' words reveal hypocrisy,[45] but rather that they are suggestive of his partial standpoint, which he strives to present as impartial, and of the complex motivation which dictates his action.[46] Consequently, even before the *agôn* the audience are invited both to sympathize with him as the victim of injustice and also to see his faults.[47]

In the *agôn* scene he speaks first (469-96) as he is the plaintiff. Although the audience now hear for the first time that he is willing to withdraw if Eteocles agrees to give him his share in the rule (484-91), his offer is matched by the threat against Thebes if Eteocles refuses to satisfy his demand. Thus, once again, the threat lurking over Thebes casts its shadow over Polynices' claims. His speech both opens (469-72) and ends (494-6) by attacking deceptive rhetoric and by claiming that he speaks the plain truth. But although the association between simplicity and truth is traditional as well as an attack against the sophists' high evaluation of rhetoric and their belief in the relativity of truth, Polynices' argument that justice is clear and accessible reveals his subjective as well as simplistic view of justice.[48] In other words, he is trapped in a course of thinking where he recognizes only his view as just and is blinded as to

the issue of his injustice in being determined to sack his homeland for the sake of his cause. This becomes more poignant
when he both decides to kill Eteocles (621) and thus incur the
guilt of fratricide, and transfers the responsibility for the sack
of Thebes to his brother (629). His invocations of the gods are
ironically reversed by Eteocles, who asks him to pray to the
Argive gods (608). This will be recalled when the Messenger
quotes Polynices' prayer to Hera, the goddess of Argos, for
support before the duel (1364-8).

His name is interpreted by Eteocles as nomen-omen: he is
Polynices of much strife (636-7). Antigone too will later deplore
the fact that her brother was aptly named (1494). This play on
the etymology was used by Aeschylus in his *Seven against
Thebes* twice by Eteocles (577-7, 658) and once after their
deaths by the Chorus (830ff.), who in a remarkable phrase
('true to their name and 'men of strife' indeed') mingles both
brothers under the name (cf. Sophocles' *Antigone* 110-11). It
will be at the end of his life that Polynices arouses the audience's sympathy not only by his emotional appeals but also by
his saying with regard to Eteocles: 'a friend (*philos*), he became
foe; but still he was friend' (1445). The ancient term *philos* is a
general term which can imply blood-relation as well as affection. Here Polynices' saying is a bitter and painful conclusion to
his life and represents the kind of enlarged understanding and
wisdom one might achieve shortly before death.

Eteocles

Eteocles' first appearance (446-51) indicates that he has grudgingly accepted his mother's invitation and his haste implies that
he does not intend to give the reconciliation attempt proper
attention. He employs the sophistic rhetoric which believes in
the relativism of values and in the power of speech to argue
both sides of a single case. By recalling the Protagorean 'man is
the measure of all things', he assertively places his own standpoint at the centre of his discussion and confidently states that
he would do anything possible to possess tyranny (absolute

power), which he personifies and considers to be the greatest of gods (504-6). His rationalizations are rich in sophistic echoes: The terms 'greater' and 'lesser' that he uses, which are later picked by Jocasta, are meant to recall the terminology used by sophists like Callicles or Thrasymachus to refer to human striving for acquisitions and his doctrine that 'it is unmanliness for one to lose the greater and get the lesser share' (509-10) recalls similar claims by these two sophists.[49]

In his eagerness to start the war because he will never give up tyranny, his supreme goal (521-3), he is unmasked as a failed leader of the state, as he shows no hesitation in endangering the communal safety. When he says that it would bring shame to him and disgrace to Thebes if Polynices were to come and take power (510-14), his phraseology reveals that he is not concerned with the beleaguered Thebes but with his own success. Similarly, he identifies the city with his cause whereas he behaves as a statesman who places his own egotistical preoccupations above the safety of the city. Even his criticism of Polynices' decision to bring a foreign army instead of opting for negotiation (515-17) is devoid of substance: if Eteocles had ever been open to negotiation he would have listened to Polynices' earlier offer to withdraw his army (484-9). After all, he tacitly concedes that he has done injustice in depriving his brother of his due share (524-5).

The dialogue between Eteocles and Creon on the theme of military tactics[50] in the second episode (690-783) may be read as a reversal of the Aeschylean dialogue between Eteocles and the Scout in the *Seven against Thebes*; whereas the Aeschylean Eteocles demonstrated his strategic ability, the Euripidean scene reveals Eteocles' practical deficiencies in the military abilities required of a leader as each plan of attack he comes up with (ambush, 724, attack at meal-time, 728, cavalry charge, 732) is rejected in turn as ineffective by Creon, who from the outset (713) hints at Eteocles' lack of stategic foresight and attributes it to his youthfulness. This is a reference not so much to the age of Eteocles (in the play he is older than Polynices) as to his inexperience and overall naiveté.

Eteocles' wish to kill his brother in battle (75) highlights his moral failure. Even his later offer, narrated by the Messenger, to avoid bloodshed of the armies and settle the issue by means of a duel (1225-34) does not show real concern for the safety of the Thebans but is rather dictated by his ardent wish to engage in single combat with Polynices and kill him. For this reason he refers to the outcome of the combat in terms of who turns out to have the rule over Thebes, and is indifferent to what happens to the Thebans in the event of his death. What the audience hear then is not about Eteocles' generous offer for the sake of his people but about his pursuit of his lust for power through intended fratricide. His silence and tearful eyes in the emotional scene of his death are left to the audience to interpret, perhaps as an indication that he too, like his brother, reached a wider understanding only at the very end of his life.

Creon

The second episode contributes to the characterization of Creon as a figure capable in military affairs but also lacking in moral wisdom, as he cautions Eteocles for his rashness in war but not for his eagerness to kill his brother. The third episode (834-1018) even questions his ability as a proper statesman and ironically parallels him to Eteocles. Like Eteocles earlier (560), so Creon here (952) faces a dilemma between his private concern and the civic interest and in the end he chooses the former at the expense of the latter. In this sense, Creon's phrase 'let the city go' (919) echoes Eteocles' very similar 'let the whole house be damned' (624).

The audience are probably meant to sympathize with Creon when he hesitates to sacrifice his own son for the sake of the city. But Euripides invites the audience to think that though parental love is universal, the love for one's homeland ought perhaps to be stronger. The closest example which sharply undermines Creon's claim comes from Euripides' *Erechtheus*.[51] In fact, there may be a deliberate allusion to this play at the beginning of the encounter between Creon and Tiresias:

Tiresias says that he is back from his journey to the land of the Erechtheids (Athens) whom he made victorious in their war with Eumolpus who attacked them with his Thracian army (852-7). In this war too, which is thus a defensive war as in *Phoenician Women*, a prophecy demanded that king Erechtheus should sacrifice one of his daughters to secure the salvation of his city. What is more important in this parallel is the reaction of Praxithea, the mother of the daughter who was sacrificed. She sets all emotions aside and in a patriotic outburst agrees to sacrifice her daughter (*TrGF* 360, *Erechtheus*). Her patriotism became exemplary, as shown by the way in which the orator Lycurgus introduces it in his Speech *Against Leocrates* (100). The contrast with Creon is sharp and becomes sharper if we think of the reversal of gender relations: instead of the typically feminine effusion of emotion Praxithea advocates the predominance of the city, whereas Creon, the male representative of the polis, subordinates communal safety to his private interest.

In the scene[52] between Creon, Antigone and Oedipus in the *exodos*, where Creon, as the nominated successor of Eteocles, enacts this role in a way which mechanically tries to put Eteocles' instruction in action, it is implied to the audience that he does not have the moral wisdom to view the circumstances following fratricide judiciously. At the same time, his decisions do not simply obey Eteocles' orders but enlarge them in a way which implies that he considers himself the ruler who can do what he wants now that Eteocles is dead. He remains blind to Antigone's sensible remark that instructions should not be carried out if they are immoral and wrong (1649). His refusal to allow Antigone to tend to her dead brother sharply and ironically contrasts with his earlier concern that Jocasta should tend to his dead son, which is followed by the maxim that 'for to the dead the living should give honour and revere the god of the underworld' (1319-20).

This contrast casts an unfavourable light over his prohibition to Antigone, similar to the role of his Sophoclean counterpart in *Antigone*, and shows him reduced to a figure of narrow-minded perception similar to that of the unyielding Eteocles earlier.

3. Characters and Actions

Similarly, he claims that his decision to send Oedipus in exile is based on Tiresias' clear statement that the city would never prosper if Oedipus remained in the land (1590-1). But Tiresias only implied that it was dangerous for the city to be ruled by one of Oedipus family and associated the civic danger with the curse of Oedipus against his sons (874-80, 886-8). Now that the fratricide has been accomplished, Oedipus' curse is no longer threatening to the city. Therefore, Creon's argument is revealed as a product of his own personal reasoning and not of Tiresias' instigation.

Tiresias and Menoeceus

The intertextual allusion to the Sophoclean Tiresias (see Chapter 2), combined with the reference to the prophet's recent help to the Ereichtheids in their war (852-5), Eteocles' request for his help (766-8) and Creon's non-questioning of the truth of his prophetic diction (962-76), are elements which contribute to the audience's reception of Tiresias as an authoritative voice in the play. Tiresias dictates that Creon's son, Menoeceus, who is the last unmarried descendant of the *Spartoi* ('The Sown Men'), must be sacrificed in propitiation of Ares' anger at Cadmus' killing of the dragon. This aspect of the Theban past, which is associated with the Theban autochthony, is not referred to by any character until this point. Jocasta in the prologue expands on the Theban past, but although she starts with Cadmus as the progenitor of the family which leads to Oedipus, she makes no reference to Cadmus' association with the other side of the Theban origin which leads to the *Spartoi*, the dragon and finally to Ares. The only allusion to this side is by the name of her father, Menoeceus, who is the descendant of the *Spartoi*.[53] On the other hand, references to this side are made regularly in the choral odes (see Chapter 4), each of which supplements the previous one by adding information about this myth, (*parodos*: 232, 1st *stasimon*: 638-75, 2nd *stasimon*: 818-21), while the Chorus also use the name Ares as a metonymy both for war and for the god.

Menoeceus' assuming a speaking part after a long silence (from line 834 down to line 976) comes as a surprise, if the audience have been led to think that he would remain a silent character throughout the scene (see Chapter 5), and hints at the active role he will soon take. Compared to both Eteocles and Polynices as well as Creon, Menoeceus is the only character who sets the civic interest above his private advantage. He refers to the Theban warriors who will not fear to fight and die in defence of their country (999-1002) in a way which implies that he wishes to align himself with them, the innocent inhabitants of Thebes, who are prepared to die although they are 'free from prophecy and not brought to divine constraint'. One may read here an implied contrast between the Theban people, who confront danger through no fault of their own and will fight to the death for their city, and Eteocles, who will fight to satisfy his lust for power and thus risks the safety of his people by dragging them to a war which he could have prevented.

Menoeceus' phraseology also includes a hint to his difference with Polynices. He envisages his life outside Thebes if he chooses voluntary exile and rejects this option because he will appear to be a base person anywhere he goes. The word *kakos* (1005) that he uses (1005) can signify cowardice (like *deilos* in 1004) but also moral failure. The idea here may thus evoke the image of Polynices in exile.[54] Polynices' preoccupation was with regaining his patrimony and no matter how understandable it was in terms of his aristocratic code it is now made to seem egotistical, as it implies that Polynices, contrary to Menoeceus here, does not grasp the moral wisdom that would have led him to place the safety of Thebes above his private interest.

A leader's responsibility for his people was a *topos* of the Homeric epic, and sacrificing one's life for the safety of one's country was already a *topos* in the protreptic elegy of the archaic period; but the juxtaposition between private and communal interest became a focus in the political discourse of the fifth century, evident in the numerous passages in Thucydides[55] and well summarized in Pericles' *Epitaphios* ('Funeral oration' in

Thucydides 2.60.2-3), where individuals may prosper when the community prospers and not vice versa. Euripides thus dramatizes a sharp juxtaposition between private and communal interest, which was a recurrent topic of the political discourse of the fifth century. Menoeceus' final verses[56] are an exhortation which encompasses this wisdom and expresses it in an arguably metatheatrical way: as in the part of a comedy where the spectators are addressed (*parabasis*), these verses seem almost to break the dramatic illusion and teach the audience that if each and every individual contributed something good to his country then countries would prosper in the future. This exhortation is in fact reminiscent of the similar words of Praxithea in *Erechtheus* (*TrGF* 360): 'My homeland, I wish that all inhabitants loved you as I do: then we would dwell in you untroubled. And you would never be subjected to harm'.[57]

The figure of Menoeceus is an example of the Euripidean tendency to idealize the innocence of young characters in dramatic worlds which are characterized by corruption. The sacrifice of a young person in particular, which develops into heroic self-sacrifice for a higher cause, is a recurrent Euripidean plot-pattern, used in *The Children of Heracles*, *Hecuba*, *Erechtheus* and *Iphigenia at Aulis*).[58] The role of Menoeceus' self-sacrifice is sometimes diminished by critics who argue that this episode is isolated, only passing references are made to it subsequently and especially as the escalation of the war between Thebans and Argives seems to invest Menoeceus' effectiveness with a certain irony.[59] But Menoeceus' self-sacrifice was followed by the eventual salvation of Thebes as Tiresias had predicted, while the grim escalation of violence only highlights the problematic consequences of the brothers' mutual killing. If inadequate emphasis is made on Menoeceus' gesture this is because the development of the dramatic plot required the treatment of fratricide and its aftermath. On another level, the lack of emphasis may be said to indicate not the ineffectiveness of Menoeceus' sacrifice but rather the gap between the idealistic worldview of characters like Menoeceus and the grim reality of the people who generate crisis.

Oedipus

Even before his appearance, the audience are invited to sympathize with Oedipus. Jocasta stresses his innocence in the prologue, while Tiresias criticizes his confinement in the palace as wrong, as this dishonourable mistreatment turned him into a savage person and caused him to curse his sons (874-7). Oedipus' curse, which sets the action into a predetermined course resulting in fratricide, is thus caused by both brothers' lack of sense (874). But at the same time Oedipus is ultimately responsible, as his cursing suggested that he acts spontaneously. This is reminiscent of the proud and rash Oedipus who acted instinctively and killed Laius (37-44). Oedipus' emotional turmoil is evident in his longing for his sons while he simultaneously curses them (327-36) as well as in his contemplating suicide. The means for killing himself, that is, either by the sword (masculine) or by hanging (feminine), reveals Oedipus' helpless 'effeminization',[60] which is also implied to the audience from the very beginning by the references to his confinement within the house. The gender inversion in the case of Oedipus suggests his helplessness and recalls a similar inversion in the case of Jocasta, where she had to take on responsibilities normally belonging to men.

His present helplessness, starting from his very physical appearance on stage as a blind old man walking with a staff (1539), as well as his exposition of his doomed past (1595-614) are meant to cause an emotional reaction in the audience. His despair at the prospect of exile is also meant to make the audience sympathize with him, while his courageous attitude, which reveals an admirable dignity, must be appealing to them: even in the depth of his despair, he refuses to supplicate Creon and appear to be a coward (1622-3). His dignity is expressed in his determination not to betray his nobility (1623-4) as well as in his attempt to dissuade his daughter from sharing in his troubles (1683-91). In the end, apart from the important companionship that Antigone offers him in his wanderings, Oedipus' hope originates from his enlarged understanding of the divine workings, as he realizes the fulfilment of an oracle given by Apollo (1703), and the prospect of the Athenian Colonus as the end of his wanderings and his suffering.

The Tutor

The Tutor is one of the ordinary people whom Euripides tends to invest with straightforwardness, honesty and moral excellence (see Chapter 1). He may be said to belong to the category of the 'simple-minded' (as contrasted to the sophisticated) people who Polynices argued would understand his cause (496). This is indeed true of the Tutor, who, at this early moment of the drama, remarks that Polynices has come to Thebes with justice and expresses the fear that the gods may view it accordingly (154-5). But this does not mean that the Tutor supports Polynices' attack; he is a Theban and as eager as Antigone and the rest of his folk to see his country prevail (154). Euripides uses the Tutor's viewpoint to show that the ordinary Theban person can understand what neither Eteocles nor Polynices accepts, that is, that there is some kind of injustice suffered by Polynices but that the intended attack endangers the safety of an entire city.

If the Tutor's ordinary wisdom helps him grasp the essence of the political crisis in Thebes, another aspect of this wisdom raises an issue that the course of the dramatic action will ironically reverse. His concluding words (196-201), motivated by the entrance of the female Chorus, reflect the misogynistic belief that the female sex causes nothing but trouble and is in general dangerous for the polis. The Tutor's view here recalls the attitude of the Aeschylean Eteocles at the beginning of *Seven against Thebes*. In that play Aeschylus juxtaposed the composed leader of the state to the terrified women of the Chorus. Aeschylus too used irony in the sense that the development of his plot gave the Chorus the kind of wisdom that was lacking in Eteocles, when they tried to convince him that the intended fratricide was wrong. In the *Phoenician Women*, Euripides gives an even sharper emphasis to the importance of female voices at times of political crisis, when male representatives of power fail in their expected role. Thus, not only will the female Chorus have wise things to convey (see Chapter 4), but the drama will show female characters, that is, Jocasta and Antigone, to be possessors of sane thinking and to take decisive part in the action.

Antigone

The Teichoskopia scene of the prologue (88-201) presents Antigone as a young girl, typically secluded within the safety of her house. Her appeals to Hecate (identified with Artemis, 109-10) and to Artemis herself (152, 191-2), which show Antigone's concern for the safety of her city, are made specifically to virgin-goddesses. Artemis is also the goddess who oversees the ritual transition of young maidens into adulthood. In metaphorical terms, the play will dramatize a transition of Antigone from her early sheltered childhood to a more independent and mature state through her gradual reaction to the circumstances she finds herself in. The gender inversion denoted in spatial terms in Antigone's exit from the house during this scene is repeated at the end of the fourth episode, when she is urged by Jocasta to accompany her to the battlefield in a final attempt to prevent fratricide (1264-83). In this scene Antigone still has a secondary and passive role; she is the secluded maiden, who hesitates to leave the women's apartments and shrinks from the crowd. In the Messenger's narrative, by contrast (1427-65), Antigone rushes up with her mother to the battlefield, joins her in lamentation, hears Polynices' request that he should be granted burial, and eventually witnesses the deaths of her brothers and the suicide of her mother over them.

In the rest of the drama Antigone resembles her mother, in a way which suggests that after her mother's death the burdens of the family are to be carried by her.[61] She releases her grief in a deeply emotional monody (1485-538), mirroring that by Jocasta in the first episode (301-54). Contrary to her passive role at the beginning of the play, she takes a leading role in her exchange with both Oedipus and Creon in the *exodos*. Reversing the pattern of her exchange with the Tutor, she now offers Oedipus both background information about the events that have taken place and support and guidance to help him end his despair. In her rational confrontation with Creon, in particular, she recalls Jocasta's competent skill in argumentation. She is presented as a mature and courageous interlocutor, who takes the initiative to speak on behalf of her family (cf. 1643-5), capable of challenging Creon's narrow standpoint (cf. 1647-9) on the question of Polynices' burial and not hesitating to voice her determination to bury her brother even if the city forbids it (1657).

Her defiant repudiation of Creon's interdict resembles that of her Sophoclean counterpart in *Antigone* and here her courage is reinforced by her determination to oppose all if necessary in order to achieve the burial of Polynices.[62] She is eager to carry out her brother's final request, and now that her mother is dead the responsibility lies entirely on her. But she finally gives up her resolve to bury Polynices in favour of accompanying her father in exile.[63] Thus, she gradually retreats in the face of Creon's obduracy (by asking him to at least let her wash the body or bandage the wounds, 1664-9) and eventually she kisses Polynices (1671) in a symbolic act which closes the theme of Polynices' burial and denotes the break of the Euripidean version from tradition.

The idea of Antigone following her father into exile is a Euripidean innovation, later elaborated by Sophocles in his *Oedipus and Colonus*, where both Antigone and Ismene join their father, and the transition from one theme (burial) to the other (help in exile) is the indication of a deliberate deviation from precedents. The abandonment of the idea of burying her brother is not meant to detract from Antigone's favourable presentation,[64] but rather to shift the emphasis onto a new theme, that is, her resolve to join her father in exile. Euripides includes another example of Antigone's defiant character as if to draw the audience's attention to the fact that Antigone remains courageous throughout: this is her refusal to marry

Creon's son, Haemon (cf. 757-8, 1436) and her threat that if she is forced to marry she is prepared to become one the Danaid maidens (1675), an allusion to the daughters of Danaus who, all but one, killed their bridegrooms on the wedding-night. Her decision to accompany her father into exile gives her a role that recalls the supportive role that Jocasta had towards her father, while her escorting of the old blind Oedipus out of the stage in the end is meant to mirror the earlier escorting in and out of stage of the old and blind Tiresias by his daughter (834, 953-4). Antigone's determination to leave Thebes and her secure life in order to stand by her father is expressed by her in terms of nobility (1692), an idea that Creon too acknowledges, although he criticizes it as folly (1680), and of the glory she will acquire (1742).

The Messengers[65]

There are two Messengers, each of whom delivers two bipartite speeches. The first Messenger opens the fourth episode and his narratives are addressed to Jocasta and the Chorus. The first speech (1090-199) briefly reports Menoeceus' death and then describes the attacking army and recounts the battle between the Argives and the Thebans down to the Theban victory and the Argives' withdrawal. This Messenger is an eyewitness and a participant in the action narrated, while his perspective is often assimilated to that of his fellow-fighters, as evident in the several uses of the all-inclusive 'we' (1099, 1142, 1143, 1150, 1171, 1189, 1196) apart from the 'I' (1164, 1165).[66] This Messenger is emotionally involved as being Eteocles' assistant in battle (1073-4, 1213). Euripides here retards dramatic action and surprises his audience. At this point of the drama the audience may well expect that Menoeceus' sacrifice will be followed by a narration of the fratricide, already foreshadowed by Tiresias (880) as well as by Eteocles' and Polynices' determination at the end of the first episode (622) and constantly lurking in references to the ever-present Oedipus' curse. Up to this point then the audience may expect to hear about a fratricide following the brothers' duel at the seventh gate as Aeschylus did in his *Seven against Thebes*. The fact that the Messenger is Eteocles' comrade and has now abandoned him may additionally cause the audience to think that he has died, as Jocasta does (1072-4). The Messenger's assurance that Eteocles is alive immediately cancels audience expectation and, in narrative terms, retards the fratricide.

The emotional tie between the Messenger and Eteocles is elaborated (1209-16) in his original unwillingness to inform Jocasta of the sad news of the upcoming duel between her sons and Jocasta has to press him just as Creon had to press Tiresias in the play. This also causes surprise to the audience, as they may not have expected that the Messenger's long speech (1090-199) would actually be followed by a second (1217-63), which now recounts the brother's decision to settle their strife in single combat. There is a significant difference in the Messenger's perspective here compared to his first speech. He narrates what happens, including Eteocles' proposal in direct speech (1225-35), stressing the effect on the reactions of the Argives and the Thebans and their words of encouragement, also in direct speech, to their corresponding leaders (1244-54). Contrary to the predominance of 'we' in the previous narrative, the Messenger now does not include himself in the side which supports Eteocles but shifts the focus to 'they'.

This distance may in fact reflect the Messenger's deliberate dissociation from the decision to settle the issue by a means that will result in fratricide. He indeed makes his differentiation clear at the very beginning of his narrative, where his statement of the facts (decision for fratricide) is accompanied by a negative assessment on his part: 'your sons intended – venture most shameful – to meet in single combat apart from all the army' (1219-20). Both his concern for the family and his judicious view of the problem of fratricide are evident in his last words, exhorting Jocasta to use any means to try and avert fratricide and suffering (1259-63).

As the first Messenger probably accompanied Jocasta and Antigone to the battlefield and so did not witness the duel, the

73

Messenger who appears in the *exodos* and addresses his news to Creon and the Chorus is meant to be another person.[67] Creon's notice of his gloomy expression is a verbal signal anticipating the bad news he brings. His first speech (1356-424) narrates the duel between the brothers and the second (1427-79), separated from the first only by the Chorus' two lines, narrates the highly emotional scene of the final moments and deaths of Eteocles, Polynices and Jocasta, as well as the strife between Argives and Thebans and the eventual victory of Thebes. In the first narrative the emphasis shifts to the Thebans and Argives who attended the fight and their manifest empathy with their leaders (1370, 1388-9, 1395, 1398-9). The mention of the opposing glances of the two brothers, as they uttered their prayers to different gods, with Polynices gazing in the direction of Argos (1364) and Eteocles gazing at Athena's temple in Thebes (1372-3), is a narration of a gesture that recalls the equally opposing gazes of the brothers in the *agôn* scene and Jocasta's effort to first make them look at each other as a first step towards reconciliation (454-9).[68] The opposing direction of their gazes once again signifies the insoluble clash between them.

The narration of the entire fight brings out the symmetry of the blows (Polynices first wounds Eteocles and is wounded in turn, Eteocles mortally stabs Polynices and is mortally stabbed by him).[69] This balance suggests the likeness between the brothers. In symbolic terms, the mortal wound that Eteocles inflicts is on his brother's navel (1412), that is, the symbol of their common origin and the mortal wound Polynices inflicts on his brother is on the liver (1421), often viewed as the seat of passions, including anger.[70] Both in the balance of his narrative and in the comments he makes on the action the Messenger gradually comes across as unbiased. Thus, Polynices' prayer that he should kill his brother is explicitly criticized by the Messenger as shameful: 'asking a most shameful crown of glory, to kill his kinsman' (1369), whereas the similar prayer of Eteocles (1373-6) receives no qualification. But although this may indicate bias, one may counterargue that Polynices' prayer comes first and causes the narrator's comment, while in Eteocles' case the same disapproval must be tacitly, albeit grudgingly, acknowledged by the narrator.

Thus, in the end the Messenger implicitly both criticizes Eteocles and sympathizes with Polynices: The mention of Eteocles' fatal mistake in considering himself the winner only to be stabbed to death by Polynices may invite sympathy but also poignantly recalls the lack of caution and rashness that have characterized Eteocles throughout the play.[71] On the other hand, when Polynices is fatally wounded the Messenger sympathizes with him and calls him 'wretched' (*talas*, 1414). The central idea that fratricide is wrong but that both brothers eagerly pursue it lurks throughout the narrative as well as determines the Messenger's perspective. It is significant that he interprets his own disapproval of the intended fratricide as shared by the many onlookers who witnessed and heard Polynices' prayers: 'tears came to many at that dread destiny and they exchanged looks, meeting eyes in turn' (1370-1). This subjective 'reading' by the Messenger is the first indication that the onlookers realize the atrocity of the upcoming event which both brothers refuse to grasp.

The emotional scene between Jocasta and her dying sons (1427-59) in the second speech emphatically conveys the wrongness of fratricide as it stresses both the disastrous results, with the death of the brothers followed by Jocasta's suicide, and gives, in direct speech, Polynices' regret. Eteocles, on the other hand, says no words and the Messenger gives his own, subjective, interpretation of his tears as he heard his mother and touched her hand: ['Eteocles] uttered no speech; but from his eyes spoke with tears, so as to give a sign of love' (1440-1). It may be that his tears, if a sign of love, were addressed strictly to his mother at the time of his death and that this did not imply that he regretted his action. But his tears may equally be interpreted as both a sign of affection and regret for the outcome. In this case, if Eteocles too, like Polynices, has shown regret, then the subsequent development of the dramatic plot in the *exodos*, with Creon acting out and amplifying Eteocles' earlier instructions, with all their dire consequences for Antigone and Oedipus, is invested with further dramatic irony.

Finally, when the Messenger moves to the violent conflict that emerged between the Thebans and the Argives in the second part of his speech he uses the all-inclusive 'we' (1461, 1468, 1472, 1475) as he now clearly belongs to the side of the Thebans and narrates the events as both an eye-witness and a participant in the action narrated. The report of the eventual Theban victory is made in terms of joy and relief as the city is now safe. The Messenger's final words (1476-9) reflect the recurrent theme of the contrast between the salvation of the city and the suffering of the royal family.

*

To conclude, the relation of character and action in the play bring to the fore central dramatic concerns, which are presented to the audience from several, often contradictory, perspectives. The theme of the fraternal strife stresses the juxtaposition between individualistic aims and communal interest. Eteocles and Polynices both use arguments to support their cases but their claims are unmasked as empty rhetoric and they both turn out to be inadequate. Themes like the greed for absolute power, strife and equity are invested with political overtones and the use of sophistic and philosophical ideas evoke for the Athenian audience ideas of their own era. The play raises the issue of repetition in human life, which in the case of the brothers evokes the idea of an inescapable pattern of plight that has ruined their family for generations. The belief that wider divine workings control someone's life even before birth (as in the case of Oedipus) suggests at first that there is no space for human freedom. However, humans have responsibility for the actions, and characters find themselves in situations where they have to make choices. Eteocles, Polynices and Creon fail as statesmen both because they do not give priority to the civic interest and because they lack moral wisdom.

Recurrent themes like that of exile or the love for one's

homeland make the audience think about what homeland stands for and how both a leader and the citizens should behave. Menoeceus' self-sacrifice is the altruistic attitude which sharply contrasts with other characters' individualistic interests. This selfless act gives a solution to the crisis which the two brothers have caused. In this respect, Menoeceus' alignment with the collective body of the citizens is related to the fact that the Thebans are presented as those always ready to die for their country but also as they who understand that the fratricidal strife is wrong. Jocasta and Antigone also understand this and try to avert disaster. Gender roles are evoked and reversed in their case in order to highlight that these women in turn assume responsibilities and take initiative in situations where men have failed. The fact that they do not manage to achieve reconciliation and avert fratricide should be regarded in the context of the severity of the brother's egotistical motives and it therefore highlights the dangers inherent in the motives of both brothers.

4

The Choral Odes

The identity of the Chorus[1] is one of the innovative aspects of Euripides' *Phoenician Women*. By contrast with Aeschylus' *Seven against Thebes*, where the Chorus consisted of Theban women, the Euripidean Chorus consist of women from the distant land of Phoenicia. This is already evident from the very title of the play, which may have puzzled the audience. The title is the same as that of Phrynichus' tragedy and the first words of Euripides' Chorus (202: 'leaving the Tyrian swell, I have come') are reminiscent of the opening of the earlier tragedy, which dramatized an entirely different theme.[2] The scholia (see on 202) reflect a critical debate on Euripides' choice of Chorus, one view suggesting that he ought to have used women who are Theban and close to Jocasta, and another that he deliberately chose a foreign Chorus who would not be afraid to speak freely to Eteocles. The truth is that nowhere in the play do the Chorus openly oppose Eteocles, though of course their foreign status indeed offers them distance and impartiality. When they seem to take sides with Polynices, remarking, as the Tutor did earlier (154), that he comes 'not without justice' (258), their remark refers to the undisputed fact that Polynices has been wronged by his brother and he comes to the *agôn* having justice on his side, and makes no comment on the questionable justice of Polynices' readiness to attack his city. Overall, the Chorus function as interlocutors who participate in the episodes, as purveyors of wisdom and above all as narrators of the Theban myth in a way which constantly brings out its relevance to the dramatic present.

The Chorus' foreign identity reveals Euripides' tendency in some of his late plays (notably *Helen* and *Iphigenia among the*

Taurians) to create an exotic atmosphere, evident in his choice of distant places as his settings. This was not unprecedented, as Aeschylus in his *Suppliants* had already created a similar atmosphere. The exact nature of the Chorus' identity in the *Phoenician Women* is given in the *parodos* ('entry-song') (202-60), where they report that they have come from the Phoenician Tyre on their journey to Delphi, where they will be Apollo's temple slaves on behalf of their city. It was during this journey that they stopped at Thebes and found themselves trapped, as the Argive troops surrounded Thebes. Their coming to Thebes is explained by their kindred relation to the Thebans (*homogeneis*, 'of the same origin', 218), as Cadmus, the founder of Thebes, and Phoenix, the father of the Phoenicians, are both descendants of Agenor. Thus the Chorus are presented as both foreign and kindred, and this double identity offers them both distance and concern for the current Theban crisis: 'I have a part in these sufferings' (249). There is also another common origin shared by the Chorus and the Thebans, as Agenor was the descendant of Io (248).

Throughout the *parodos* the Chorus refer to Theban prehistory and the gods in a typically allusive manner which prepares the audience for what is to come. Strophe 1 (202-13), antistrophe 2 (214-25) and the mesode (226-38) depict Delphi (the intended end of the journey) as a sacred and blissful place of peace, security and prosperity, associated with the gods Apollo and Dionysus who reside there. At the heart of their description the Chorus mention the 'holy caves of the dragon', a reference to the well-known myth according to which Apollo's founding of the oracle at Delphi followed his killing of Python, the dragon who guarded the place. This myth generally signifies the birth of order and civilization following the annihilation of the primordial chaos and violence associated with the dragon's chthonic powers.[3] The passing allusion that is made to it here will be elaborated by the Chorus later in a way which will suggest to the audience its relevance to events at Thebes. The stark transition (*nun de*, 'but now', 239) to strophe 2 (239-49) reverses the image of serenity as both here and in antistrophe

2 (250-60) the Chorus refer to Ares as the god of war and also the metonymy of war: Ares 'has come' (*molôn*, 240) to bring war to the city and will witness the outcome. The contrast between Apollo and Dionysus as the gods of quiet bliss on the one hand and Ares as the god of disaster and confusion on the other is sharp. The disastrous effect of Ares is said by the Chorus to also bring the 'woe of the Furies' to Oedipus' sons. Here the menace presented by Ares is associated with the workings of Oedipus' curse on his sons and the audience are invited to think that Polynices' bringing of the foreign army to his homeland is under the influence of Oedipus' curse.

The first *stasimon* (638-89) resumes[4] themes of the *parodos* and takes them one step further by adding more information on the Theban prehistory. At the heart of this ode is the coming of the Tyrian Cadmus to the land and the founding of the city of Thebes. There is a parallel created between the women of the Chorus and Cadmus, as both are Tyrians, and both leave their country and travel to Thebes. Cadmus' settlement of the city is divinely ordered and is described in terms reminiscent of the description of Delphi in the parodos. Cadmus' Thebes is a land of prosperity where Dionysus, the god of bliss, was borne and later worshipped (strophe 1). The implicit parallel between Thebes and Delphi turns into an implicit parallel between Apollo and Cadmus in the antistrophe (657-75), as the narration of the founding of the city is reminiscent of Apollo's founding of the oracle. Cadmus too had to kill the murderous dragon that guarded the area and, following a divine command, sowed the dragon's teeth from which sprang the armed Sown Men who killed one another.

Cadmus was assisted by Athena (666, 1062), who later was worshipped in Thebes, and in the course of the play Eteocles prays to this goddess for help prior to the duel (1373). According to myth, not all of the Earth-borne (the *Spartoi*) perished but some lived and helped Cadmus found the city. It was from them that the autochthonous line of Creon descended, with Menoeceus being the youngest descendant. The autochthnonous descent was regarded both as honourable, since it was evidence of the old origin of the city, and as negative, since it referred back to the savage dragon who was killed by Cadmus, as the Chorus will explain by the use of the oxymoron 'most glorious shame' (*kalliston oneidos*, 821) in the second *stasimon*.[5] In the myth it is significant that the dragon is Ares' son (658) and it this detail that Euripides exploits for dramatic effect, as becomes explicit in Tiresias' revelation of the oracle in the third episode. As Tiresias explains (931-41), in order to appease Ares' wrath for the ancient killing of the dragon a child descended from the race of the Sown Men must be sacrificed. This sacrifice will win Ares as an ally for the Thebans. In fact, Euripides uses Ares almost as a recurrent motif[6] in this play to exploit the dynamics both of the general metonymy for war and of the god's personal involvement.

This emphasis on Ares indicates a dramatic exploitation of a mythological detail which may have been suggested by Aeschylus. In the *Seven against Thebes*, which in Aristophanes' *Frogs* (1021) is called a drama 'full of Ares', Aeschylus refers to Ares as the traditional protector of Thebes (e.g. 105-6, 135ff.). His protection of Thebes was the result of his reconciliation with Cadmus after the slaying of the dragon, symbolically confirmed by the marriage of Cadmus with Harmonia, Ares' and Aphrodite's daughter. This marriage is referred to by Jocasta in the prologue (7), where Harmonia is named only as the daughter of Aphrodite. This may be a dexterous suppression of Ares so that his actual role will be gradually revealed to the audience. Jocasta's reference to these past events at the very beginning of the play significantly begins the enumeration of Theban sufferings with Cadmus and not with Laius' transgression (as the scholium on 4 remarks). So already at the beginning of his play Euripides alludes to something that will become apparent to the audience gradually: Cadmus is the important founder and benefactor of Thebes, as he kills the chthonic dragon and initiates the life of the city, but at the same time he is the one who, by slaying the dragon, causes the wrath of Ares which dogs the Thebans for generations to come.

Although Cadmus, the dragon and Ares were of course

present in accounts of the Theban prehistory, neither Aeschylus nor Sophocles exploited the consequences of the slaying of the dragon for dramatic effect.[7] By contrast, Euripides focused on Ares' role in the events[8] and chose to dramatize a version according to which the reconciliation between Cadmus and the god failed and Ares' wrath remained unappeased. The idea of the failure of a reconciliation is of course central in the play and dramatized in Eteocles' and Polynices' fierce confrontation first in words and then in the battlefield. At the same time, the emphasis on the myth of the foundation of the city also evokes the idea of civil strife as the Earth-born killed one another, a fratricidal tendency that is shared also by the two brothers[9] and only Menoeceus' sacrifice points in the direction of the civic salvation. Eteocles' and Polynices' violent clash recalls details of the prehistory of Thebes, either of the Sown Men or even of Cadmus: during the duel, Eteocles throws a piece of rock against his brother (1401) as Cadmus did against the dragon (663). The word used (*marmaron*) for the rock is the same. At the same time, the two brothers are often likened to wild animals (1380, 1573) in a way that is reminiscent of the Homeric usage, which emphasizes the warriors' strength, but also underlines their savage ferocity, which makes the Chorus call them 'twin beasts' (1296) in the fourth *stasimon*, and which gives them a sort of bestial nature reminiscent of the dragon and, as will become apparent later, of the Sphinx.

The Chorus' invocations in the epode (676-89) of Io and Epaphus (the son of Io and Zeus) as well as of Persephone, Demeter, and Gê (Earth) are made in the form of a hymn inviting a god to appear, and have an apotropaic aim similar to Antigone's invocation of Leto, Hecate, Artemis and Selene in the Teichoskopia scene. The reference to Epaphus as 'offspring of (our) ancestress' (676-7) recalls the mention of Io in the parodos and enhances the idea of the Chorus' kindred relation with the Thebans.

There is also an implicit contrast between Thebes having Io as a protector and Argos having Hera, Io's persecutor, as a patron goddess (albeit also a local deity in Thebes, cf. 24), ironically invoked by Polynices for help at a time when he seems to have been assimilated by Argos (1365-8). On a second level however, the emphasis on Io as the remote ancestor, combined with the reference to Epaphus,[10] may allude to another genealogy: according to myth, Epaphus and Io were the ancestors not only of the Phoenicians and Thebans via Agenor but also of the Argives via Danaus. It may be not accidental that the Argive troops in the play are often called Danaan or Danaid (430, 466, 860, 1226, 1245). On the other hand, the Thebans are often called Cadmeans (1227, 1239, 1399, 1467). This may be a deliberate reminder to the audience that the Thebans and the Argives, now enemies, have common origins, a fact which casts a dark shadow over their war. At the same time, there is irony in the invocation of Gê (Earth) as the nurturer of all, as, according to Tiresias' oracle (939), the Theban earth in the play, which gave birth to the dragon (818-21, 931, 935), wants to be appeased, along with Ares, by means of the sacrifice of one descendant of the earth-born dragon.

The contrast between Ares as the bringer of war and disaster and Dionysus as associated with peace and prosperity informs strophe 1 of the second *stasimon* (784-832), which ends with the image of Eris (the personification of strife), dreadful goddess who has brought woe to the royal house. Traditionally *eris* (strife) is associated with Ares (as the god of war) but the specific reference here evokes the particular strife between the brothers[11] and recalls the association of Ares with Oedipus' curse in the *parodos* (250-5). The invocation of Cithaeron, the mountain associated with the fate of the infant Oedipus, is followed by a reference to the Sphinx, first mentioned by Jocasta in the prologue (46). The reference to the Sphinx (806-10) as the monster 'with most unmusical songs' (807)[12] who came to Thebes and caused death to the Thebans recalls[13] the image of Ares in antistrophe 1, where he is described as the converse of Dionysus, that is, as a god who has no relation with music but causes death instead. Like the dragon in the remote past, so the Sphinx in the recent past represents the monstrous powers that are subdued by a saviour hero and benefactor, so that two corresponding parallels are established, one between the dragon and the Sphinx and another between Cadmus and Oedipus.

The underlying similarity of the Sphinx with Ares in terms of their negation of music and peace, strengthened by the fact that the Sphinx as Ares causes death to the Thebans, invites the audience to think that the present strife, associated with Ares, is yet another stage in the long Theban tradition where peace and prosperity are threatened.[14] As the Chorus remark, 'what is not good never gave rise to good' (814), that is, the evil in Oedipus' family perpetuates itself through generations. The epode refers to the earth-born dragon as an ambiguous element in the pre-history of Thebes ('most glorious shame', 821), and to the wedding of Harmonia and Cadmus, which recalls the remote happy past, and ends with an invocation of Io.

The relevance of the third *stasimon* to the action has often been questioned.[15] A scholium on 1019 condemns it as entirely irrelevant, remarking that, although one might expect the Chorus to focus on Menoeceus, instead they narrate the events about Oedipus and the Sphinx which have been mentioned repeatedly. But a close look at the *stasimon* reveals that Menoeceus comes to the foreground as the climactic saviour of his homeland. Strophe 1 stresses the calamity imposed by the Sphinx and strophe 2 presents Oedipus as the subduer of the monster and the rescuer of Thebes, albeit paying a deeply ironic service to the city, as through his incest he turned from saviour into a destroyer. The mention of Menoeceus in strophe 2 is meant to compare him with Oedipus (note the use of the epithet *kallinikos*,[16] 'gloriously victorious' for both, 1048, 1059, although in the case of Oedipus it is ironic as later at 1728-31) but shows that by contrast with Oedipus Menoeceus proved a true rescuer of his city. His patriotic self-sacrifice makes him a true *kallinikos*, just as another sacrifice, that of Erechtheus' daughter, alluded to by Tiresias, made the Athenians *kallinikous* (855). The Chorus' wish that they should be blessed with children like Menoeceus heightens the praise of Menoeceus but also recalls

Menoeceus' wish that future generations similarly would prove their love to their homeland.

The reference to the 'seizing' of Cadmeans as the act of the Sphinx, referred to at the beginning of the *stasimon* (1021, cf. 46), is used at the very end of the *stasimon* to refer to the divine destruction that fell on Thebes as a sequel to Cadmus' slaying of the dragon. The joining of the Sphinx with the dragon which frames the *stasimon* may be a deliberate attempt to imply that Thebes had a troubled relation with the gods and constantly oscillated between prosperity and calamity.[17] The references for example to Apollo and Pallas Athena as the helper of Cadmus in the killing of the dragon eventually turned into a sequence of disaster when Cadmus caused the wrath of Ares and Earth. The vague reference to the gods recalls Jocasta's reference in the prologue to Apollo's prohibition to Laius to beget children 'against gods' will' (18. Note that both here and at 1066 the word *daimon* is used, a term which vaguely describes some divine power). Apollo there does not say that it is he who does not want Laius to beget children but attributes this to divine powers.[18] Oedipus too, in his *excursus* on his past credits Apollo only with the oracle that he should kill his father (1598-9).[19]

There is, then, the idea emerging that there are divine powers operating both in the case of Oedipus' family and in the case of Theban pre-history (with the role of Ares being of primary importance) that influence the development of the events. But the play constantly reminds the audience that along with divine influence, either personal (in the form of a god) or impersonal (such as fate), humans too bring on themselves avenging spirits through their acts, as Oedipus' patricide and incest brought upon him a disastrous sequel or his sons' mistreatment of their father brought upon them the curse which doomed them to death. The way the characters themselves personify and deify abstract ideas sometimes reveals their tendency to promote their own motives at the expense of traditional gods. When Eteocles, for example, deifies Tyrannis (royal power) he reveals a theistic approach which only betrays his egoistic motives. Overall, although the exact nature of divine involvement in human affairs is vague, the play makes human responsibility the focus of attention. For example, both the brothers and Menoeceus are trapped within a constraint imposed upon them, that is, that of the curse and that of the oracle respectively, but the different way in which they respond reveals their difference: the brothers show their egotism whereas Menoeceus' voluntary self-sacrifice demonstrates his altruistic motives.

In the third *stasimon* the Sphinx's murderous destruction of the Thebans is meant to recall the association of Ares both with the dragon and with the current war. The emphasis on the Sphinx's murders of young people, in particular, recalls Tiresias' oracle that required the sacrifice of a young person, while the emotionally strong description of the female lamentations every time the Sphinx snatched a Theban both resembles the laments at the time of war as foretold by Tiresias (883) and looks back to Antigone's fear of women being dragged to slavery (185-92) and forward to Antigone's bitter lamentation (1485-538).

The brief fourth *stasimon* foretells fratricide and becomes a dirge in anticipation. Both brothers are mingled in a duality which suggests their similarity ('murderous spirits, twin beasts', 1296-7).[20] This imagery[21] links them with the Sphinx, the monster who brought disaster to Thebes. Although Ares is not named, his ever-present role is implied when the Chorus say that 'this day will decide the future', and that the Furies, too, are instrumental in the coming slaughter (1306). This pairing recalls the end of the *parodos*, where the Chorus said that Ares would soon decide the outcome of the battle bringing to Oedipus' sons the woe of the Furies (250-5). The sons of Oedipus are not simply under the influence of Ares and the curse, but they are also described in terms suggestive of their incorporation of Ares: The Chorus' description of both brothers as 'murderous' souls used the epithet *phonios*, which in the course of the play has been associated with the savagery of the dragon (657) and of Ares (*phoinion*, 1006).

86

The Chorus' reference to the fear and the pity they feel (1284-8) recalls Aristotle's famous discussion of Greek tragedy's arousal of these two central emotions among the spectators.[22] But even before Aristotle critics like Gorgias (*Helen* 9) referred to poetry's arousal of these emotions in the audience. Hence, apart from the understandable sympathizing of the Chorus with the suffering of Jocasta, the mention of these emotions at this point may have the additional function of a metatheatrical reference to the reaction of the audience. After all, the audience share with the Chorus the status of being detached from the events but also familiar with the mythological background, distanced but also emotionally involved in the dramatic plot.[23]

*

To sum up, the Chorus' double identity in the play, as both foreign and kindred, both distances them from and involves them in the dramatic action. The choral odes contribute to the interpretation of the dramatic events by establishing links between the remote myth and the dramatic present. The failure of reconciliation between the brothers recalls the unresolved friction between Ares and Cadmus and their fratricidal strife makes them similar to the *Spartoi*. Their bestial nature also links them both to the chthonic dragon and to the Sphinx, in a way which implies that they are a threat to the city of Thebes. The choral odes also suggest the presence of divine powers influencing the Theban family throughout its history. But humans are responsible for their actions. In the case of the brothers, this means that they may be under the influence of Ares or their father's curse, yet their decisions and actions are their own responsibility throughout.

5

Performance

Performance criticism[1] is an area of study which attempts to explore the relation between the written script and the theatrical spectacle in order to try and reconstruct some degree of the original performance as well as to investigate the possibilities of the text for modern productions. In what follows, I shall discuss some performative aspects of the play and their contribution to its interpretation, by focusing on the explicit or implicit stage directions embedded in the text and the potentialities offered by the text for staging.

The second hypothesis to the play notes that it has a large cast. Apart from the eleven speaking characters several silent extras[2] appear on stage: Eteocles' attendants in the first (261-637) and second (690-783) episodes, Tiresias' daughter in the third episode (834-1018), as well as attendants carrying the corpses in the *exodos* (1308-766). The play is rich in parts demanding both speaking and singing by the actors, which requires a high degree of ability. The rule of the three actors, which determines the distribution of several characters among three actors, makes the allocation of parts more difficult, as the actors have singing parts: These include monodies (301-54, 1485-538) and lyric exchanges between actors or between actors and the Chorus (182-92, 1340-51, 1539-81, 1710-57).

A possible allocation would be the following:[3] Actor 1 (the protagonist): Jocasta, Antigone (except for the lyrical section 1270-83) and Menoeceus. Actor 2 (the deuteragonist): Eteocles, Tiresias, the Messengers, Oedipus. Actor 3 (the tritagonist): Tutor, Polynices, Creon, Antigone (1270-82). The impersonation of both Tiresias and Oedipus by the same actor would be telling as these two characters share physical similarities and their overall appearance would evoke each other. An alternative allocation would split the Messenger parts between two actors, the second and third actors respectively. It may have also been the case that the role of Polynices was given to the deuteragonist and that of Eteocles was given to the tritagonist if one follows Demosthenes' remark in his speech *On the false embassy* (123) that the parts of the tragic kings were normally given to the tritagonists as special recompense.[4] Such an allocation would affect in turn the distribution of Creon's part, as Creon and Eteocles appear together onstage and cannot be played by the same actor, and that of Tiresias, as he also appears together with Creon onstage.

The scholium on 93 remarks that the reason behind the Tutor's appearance earlier than Antigone is a theatrical necessity, that is, time is needed for the protagonist who plays Jocasta in the monologue to change his costume and mask into the character of Antigone, whom he also plays. It would make sense for the same actor to play these two central roles, both of which call for high acting and singing abilities, especially as the two characters are made to resemble and mirror each other in the course of the play. The allocation of the part of Menoeceus also to the same actor is telling, as Menoeceus matches Jocasta and Antigone in being favourably presented to bring a solution to the present crisis.

The high degree of sung parts (both Chorus and characters) contributes to the intense and varied aural dimension of the play. The music of the original performance is lost and one can only hope to try and reconstruct the general atmosphere, with the alternation of metres and emotions.[5] The play is also characterized by the increased lyrical parts given to actors, both in monodies and in sung dialogue. Dance movements too accompany Jocasta's singing (316) in a way which brings together the aural and visual effect. Another aspect of the original performance that is lost is its stagecraft, though in this case a careful reading of the text can provide useful clues as to the overall visual dimension of the play. The third hypothesis remarks that the *Phoenician Women* is a fine play in terms of visual stage effects, which can be easily confirmed if one merely considers the use of the palace roof for the spectacular Teichoskopia scene between Antigone and the Tutor, the Chorus' exotic costumes, the impressive entrances and exits, the emotional scenes of physical contact,[6] or the presence of many characters, silent extras and props.

The dramatic time at the opening of the play is conventionally daytime and the prelude to the impending attack of the Argive troops on Thebes. The setting is Thebes and its royal palace, which is represented on stage by the *skênê*, a wooden building with a central door and a flat roof. Entrances and exits through the central door are made by Jocasta, Antigone, Oedipus and Eteocles, while entrances and exits are also made from the sides (*parodoi*), possibly with a distinction[7] made between the side that leads to the city walls and outside the city (used by Polynices, Eteocles, Creon, Menoeceus, the Messengers, Jocasta, Antigone and Oedipus) and that which leads to other locations within the Theban district (used by Tiresias, his daughter and Menoeceus, Creon and the second Messenger).

The setting in Aeschylus' *Seven against Thebes* was also the palace, but Euripides creates a quite different atmosphere. Whereas the Aeschylean play opened with Eteocles addressing a group of his townspeople, hence stressing the public aspect, the *Phoenician Women* presents Jocasta recounting direct to the audience the past and present problems of the royal family, thus emphasising the familial side. Furthermore, the interplay between internal and external, which is dramatized in the Teichoskopia scene, with Antigone and the Tutor standing on the palace roof and overlooking the military camp, evokes the complex relationship between civic and familial interest which lies at the core of the drama. In the proximity of the palace there is an altar devoted to Apollo Aguieus, which the spectators must have seen on stage, whereas readers are informed about it by Polynices' words at the end of the first episode (631). This serves as a constant reminder of Apollo's ever-present role in the Labdacid family. When Polynices enters at 274 he mentions 'the fires on the altars are near, and the shrines are not untended', and later tells his mother of his emotional reaction upon seeing the altars (367). This signifies the presence on stage of prop-altars, which remind the audience of Polynices' ambiguous relation to his country: these are the altars of the country he is ready to attack and on which he is prepared to dedicate trophies of a shameful victory (cf. 572, 624). This impression is also enhanced by references to the temples, altars and divine statues which the audience are invited to envisage in the surrounding district of Thebes (604, 632, 1372-3, 1751-2).

Apart from prop-altars (274) and statues (632), several other props are used in the play, including armour (779), swords (267, 276), Tiresias' prophetic lots (838), the staves carried by Tiresias (implied by the action in 836) and Oedipus (1539) and the dummy corpses of Eteocles, Polynices and Jocasta on biers (1693-8), probably bearing their corresponding masks. The text incorporates references to the nature of masks and costumes: Jocasta's mask is that of an old woman (302) with shorn hair and her costume is black (372-3). Antigone's mask is that of a young girl (106) and she is presented as wearing a luxurious saffron garment and a veil on her head in the first part of the drama, whereas in the *exodos* either she appears with no veil and part of her garment discarded or she is presented as actually making the change to her costume onstage (1490-1). It is possible that in the *exodos* her mask changes into that of a person in mourning. The Tutor's mask is that of an old man (107) and his garment that of a slave (94). Eteocles and Polynices are young men (1360) wearing swords (596, 267), whereas Menoeceus is presented as an adolescent (947). Tiresias and Oedipus are both aged (896, 1619), blind (834, 1539) and carry staves (836, 1539). Creon too is an old man (1318). The Messengers are soldiers (1213, 1468-9). The Chorus wear exotic and impressive costumes (278-9).[8]

Several references are made to the Theban walls and their gates (79, 114-15, 181) as well as to the Theban territory (101, 102, 111, 131) in a way which invites the audience to think of the Theban past and its dire present. Jocasta's use in her opening monologue of the demonstrative pronoun *tade* ('these', 79) to refer to these walls already marks their presence with significance. There may have actually been paintings depicting the walls around the stage to visualize the dramatic interplay between the obvious/exterior danger and the implicit/interior danger. The Tutor's reassuring remark that 'internally at least the city is secure' (117) suggests to the audience that the walls may keep the city safe from the Argive enemies but enclose the real threat, that is, the Labdacids' troubled past, which is now exemplified in the strife between Eteocles and Polynices. This impression is enhanced by means of the direction of the gaze of both Antigone and the Tutor towards the exterior, where the obvious enemy is located (see Chapter 2). Antigone's longing for Polynices, as well as the Tutor's remark on the justice of his cause, further undermine the clarity of the contrast between Thebes and enemies, as Polynices is both a friend (*philos*) and an enemy. In spatial terms, this ambivalent state of Polynices is dramatized by the fact that he will come to Thebes under truce, that is, he, an exile and an enemy, will pass into the palace through the walls that keep the Thebans and the Argives apart.

Prologue (1-201)

Jocasta enters and exits the stage through the palace door at the beginning and end of her monologue. Her exit is followed by the appearance of the Tutor and Antigone, who are first heard by the audience climbing up an unseen ladder from within the building until they actually become visible on the top of the *skênê*-building, which signifies the palace roof. The Tutor delays Antigone's appearance, as he begins to ascend the ladder first and speaks to her while she is still invisible. At 100-8 Antigone appears and remains on the palace roof until urged by the Tutor to enter the house (193). Their appearance causes surprise, as the audience were prepared by Jocasta (83) to expect the arrival of Polynices. The use of the palace roof,[9] usually a place where divine characters appear, following Jocasta's closing prayer, is

an early hint at the fact that although divine workings have
never ceased to affect the lives of the Labdacids, there will be no
divine appearances in this play; the characters as well as the
audience are called to make their own meaning of the divine
involvement in human affairs.

As the spectators can see, Antigone wears bright colours,
which is appropriate for her young age, while the reader learns
this in the *exodos*, when she changes her garment into clothes
of mourning (1490-1). The exchange (88-201) of iambic trime-
ters (Tutor) and lyric metres (Antigone) gives variation to the
overall tone and contributes to the creation of an atmosphere of
tension and excitement. The image of Antigone and the old
Tutor, where Antigone relies on him for guidance, will be
recalled at the end of the play in the image of Antigone and
Oedipus, where Antigone will acquire an active role and will be
the one to guide her old father (1710-11).

First episode (261-637)

Polynices enters through the *parodos* that leads to the exterior
(possibly left). Although his coming is foretold by Jocasta in the
opening monologue, his entrance comes as a surprise as it is
unheralded. The dramatic reason given is that his fear of
possible ambush has made him pass inside the walls secretly.
His entry is given several stage directions. He walks nervously
and cautiously with his sword drawn and ready to defend
himself from ambush, constantly looking around. The use of a
demonstrative pronoun to accompany the word 'sword' (267) is
an emphatic direction of the audience's gaze towards Polynices'
weapon, which he brandishes on stage, and in dramatic terms it
hints at the symbolic significance of the sword as a prop: it will
play, albeit off-stage, a fundamental role in the fratricide and is
also the concrete aspect of Oedipus' curse on his sons, that is, to
divide the patrimony by the iron (sword). He may wear the
flashing golden armour described by Antigone in the
Teichoskopia scene (168-9). If this is the case, his warrior-
costume would visually enhance his readiness to attack his city,

while the brightness of its colour would later contrast with Jocasta's dark clothes. He hears imaginary sounds and gradually reaches the altars and shrines as he walks towards the *orchêstra*. The reference to these sacred places may have been accompanied by a gesture of recognition and greeting (274-5). He pauses upon seeing the women of the Chorus and withdraws his sword. His identifying the Chorus as foreign (278-9) is probably a verbal recognition of the foreign nature of their costume.

The language of the Chorus is of course Greek, and the allusion to the foreign character of their speech (301, cf. 679, 1302) is a means to indicate their foreign identity. But Jocasta's reference to their 'Phoenician cry' at 301-3 may imply that the sung verses of the Chorus which precede are accompanied by an oriental melody.[10] The Chorus prostrate themselves before Polynices when they learn his identity, and this bodily movement visually signifies their foreign identity, as prostration before royalty was considered a non-Greek custom and indicative of foreigners' lack of freedom. The Chorus invite Jocasta to come out of the palace and the audience may have caught a glimpse of the interior space as the central door opens and Jocasta emerges to welcome her son. The Chorus' asking Jocasta why she is delaying to come and embrace her son may at first seem like a mere detail to cover the brief time until Jocasta's exit through the central door. At the same time, however, it may foreshadow Jocasta's significant delay later on, when she rushes to the battlefield along with Antigone to reach her sons but fails to arrive in time.

At 304 Jocasta sees Polynices. The scene that ensues is intense in both aural and visible terms: the two characters embrace and Polynices' long hair contrasts with Jocasta's shorn head (322-3). The contrast in their appearances is enhanced by Jocasta's black clothes, where the colour symbolism functions as a visual reminder of her past mourning and a hint at her future mourning as well as her death. Her sung monody is a highly emotional outburst of grief and joy as Jocasta dances around her son, probably stroking him with her hands.[11] Polynices tells his mother his reaction on returning to Thebes, which the spectators have already seen. He mentions his weeping (366-8) upon seeing his familiar places. As Altena has noted,[12] a comparison between the narrated and the enacted scene of entrance reveals that no clue is given that Polynices wept upon his entrance (261-77), and he may now be trying to win over his mother's sympathy immediately prior to the impending debate with Eteocles. Polynices also does not mention to his mother what the audience heard him saying during his entrance, namely, that he both trusts and distrusts her (272). Jocasta has no reason to doubt her son's sincerity, either in terms of his weeping or subsequently in terms of his emotional concern for his father and sisters, but different stagings of the scene may guide the audience towards different 'readings' of Polynices' character.

Eteocles (heralded by the Chorus at 443-4) enters at 446, either alone, like Polynices, or more probably accompanied by attendants as in the next episode, here to stress his possession of the royal power that Polynices has come to lay claim to. He probably enters through the same *parodos* with his brother, as he is also coming from the battlefield. Alternatively, the use of the opposite *parodos* would be an early visual hint not only of their present enmity but more generally of their entirely different worldviews. Eteocles may be wearing his armour, in which case the visual effect would enhance the notion of the impending battle, or he may be wearing a royal outfit to symbolize his unwillingness to concede monarchy and serve as a visual reminder that the fraternal strife aims at royal power. Especially in the latter case the allusions to the sceptre by both Eteocles and Polynices (591, 601) may have been not merely a metaphor for 'royal power' but also a reference to a sceptre as a prop. If the spectators saw Eteocles carrying a royal sceptre and Polynices carrying a sword, this would be a visual reminder that Eteocles clings to power and Polynices is ready to fight to get it.[13]

The verbal reference to Eteocles' fierce gaze (454) probably intensifies the facial expression indicated by the mask, while his overall posture must indicate his impatience. Jocasta urges

(454-9) her sons to look into each other's eyes, which implies that Eteocles and Polynices have been avoiding looking at each other. The text does not say whether they actually did and here the different possibilities for directing their response may contribute to their characterization and their reception by the audience, in terms of their relation to their mother and the intensity of their feelings.[14] In their speeches both characters refer to each other in the third person (474, 477, 478, 481, 511), which is in accordance with the mode of address between opponents in forensic speeches and here further enhances the impression of their estrangement. This estrangement may have been visually indicated by the two characters directing their gaze only to their mother, who as the arbitrator may have placed herself in the middle.

Jocasta turns her gaze first to Eteocles at 528 and then to Polynices at 568 to mark the beginning of the parts of her speech addressed to each of her sons in turn. At 587-93 Eteocles addresses his mother, ruling out any possibility of reconciliation and his haste may be an indication of bodily movement towards leaving. At 593 his threatening address to Polynices ('as for you: get outside these walls, or you'll die') brings the *agôn* scene to an end in a rapid and heated exchange. It may be that Eteocles' attendants, armed with swords, make their presence felt and prompt Polynices' reply that if anyone thrusts upon him a weapon he will suffer the same (594-5). Eteocles' request to his brother to notice his hands probably implies that Eteocles seizes his sword (596) and causes Polynices' mockery (Et.: 'You are near at hand, not gone far. Do you observe my hands? Po.: I see them. But wealth is cowardly, and contemptibly clinging to life, 596-7).

In this heated part of the exchange the two characters are looking at each other, only this time it is not associated with reconciliation as Jocasta had hoped in vain, but rather visually emphasizes the climax of their confrontation, which is verbally expressed through the fierce acceleration of pace. The use of *antilabê* (division of line between two speakers) and the change of the metre from the iambic trimeter into trochaic tetrameters, probably to the accompaniment of the *aulos* (flute or pipe)[15] marks a pathetic change of rhythm and creates an atmosphere of heightened verbal tension as a prequel to the duel. Polynices exits through the left *parodos* and Jocasta enters the palace though the central door. A staging that would further emphasize Eteocles' vehemence would be to make him briefly follow his brother offstage as if to make sure that he has departed.[16] Jocasta's silent entry into the palace could be marked by slow movement and a downcast gaze, to indicate the failure of her attempt at reconciliation and her despair here. Eteocles and his attendants enter the palace at 637.

Second episode (690-783)

Eteocles has either stayed on stage during the choral performance,[17] as Creon does during the second *stasimon*, or has gone into the palace at the end of the first episode, re-emerging at the opening of the second episode.[18] He orders one of his followers, who is a silent extra, to send a message to Creon. At 767 Eteocles leaves the stage. The dramatic motive of his departure is his enmity with Tiresias in the past, but his exit is conditioned also by a theatrical convention, if the same actor who plays Eteocles will have to play Tiresias in the exchange with Creon.

At the end of the episode, Eteocles calls on his attendants, that is, the silent extras present onstage, to fetch him his armour. This recalls the Aeschylean Eteocles' similar order (*Seven against Thebes* 675). His attendants may immediately respond by bringing the armour from inside the *skênê*, and Eteocles then either puts on the armour during part of the second *stasimon* and leaves through the *parodos* which leads to the battlefield, or, more plausibly, simply leaves, followed by his attendants who carry the armour.[19] The dramatic significance of Eteocles leaving the stage without wearing his armour may have been the sense that the duel may be delayed or even averted. He never appears alive again, and the actor who plays him probably returns in the next episode to play the character of Tiresias. Creon remains onstage during the second *stasimon*.

Third episode (834-1018)

Tiresias enters through the *parodos* (possibly on the right) which leads from his home in Thebes. He is blind and aged. He walks slowly and is attended to by his daughter, who carries records of prophecies, probably wooden tablets or scraps of papyrus,[20] and accompanied by Menoeceus, who remains silent. He wears a golden crown, the symbol of his prophetic ability, traverses the 'steep' (851) *parodos* and reaches the level ground of the stage. He probably has his one hand on his daughter's shoulder, as she leads the way, and in the other hand he carries a staff. The difficulty of his movement is stressed by the fact that when he finally reaches Creon he can hardly take a breath. Creon's urge to Menoeceus to assist Tiresias at 846 implies that Menoeceus probably grasps Tiresias' arm and leads him next to Creon until Tiresias can stand firm at 849. Menoeceus then stays near him (906). At that moment Tiresias may receive the prophetic lots from his daughters as holding them in hand may reinforce the validity of his diction.[21]

Menoeceus does not speak until 976. After such a long silence this probably comes as a surprise, as the audience may have thought that he would remain a mute person throughout the scene, especially since Creon replies to Tiresias on his son's behalf. It has been suggested that the reference to Tiresias' difficulty in walking and to the need for Menoeceus' help indicates the existence of steps that separate the *orchêstra* from the low-raised stage.[22] This could indeed be the case if there was a slight height-difference in the levels of these two theatrical spaces, although Menoeceus' assistance makes perfect sense, as it stresses Tiresias' old age and weakness.[23] The text at 895-6 implies that Creon attempts to prevent Tiresias from leaving, probably laying hands on him and blocking his way as the prophet attempts to leave. This scene will be recalled in the fourth episode, when Jocasta will similarly try to prevent the reluctant Messenger from leaving without revealing his news.

The revelation of the oracle that demands the sacrifice of Menoeceus was probably followed by gestures and bodily movements on Creon's part to enhance the notion of his despair. Although the text says nothing about Menoeceus' reaction at this point, the actor who plays Menoeceus may have given some indication, perhaps of shock or fear, in the first part of his dialogue with Creon, where the audience have not yet heard that he is deceiving his father into believing that he will try to save his life. At 923 Creon supplicates Tiresias, kneels before the prophet, touches his knee and extends his arm to reach his chin. Kaimio[24] argues that this supplication was not staged but only expressed verbally. However, the staging of a scene where Creon is seen by the audience supplicating Tiresias is significant, as there will be a sharp contrast when in the *exodos* Oedipus refuses to supplicate Creon or when Antigone attempts to 'supplicate' Creon invoking Jocasta.

At 953 Tiresias' encouragement to his daughter to lead the way implies that he probably places his hand on her shoulder after handing back the prophetic lots to her.[25] At 970 Creon turns to his son to arrange for the plan of escape until at 986 Menoeceus urges him to leave. Creon then probably leaves from the right *parodos* to collect money for his son's escape (or otherwise enters the palace), while Menoeceus approaches the *orchêstra* to address the Chorus, and leaves through the *parodos*. It has been suggested[26] that Menoeceus rather enters the palace to see his adoptive mother (an idea given by his earlier saying at 986-7) and perhaps also to reveal his plan to her; otherwise, the lack of reaction on Jocasta's part upon hearing the news of his death at 1090 would be difficult to comprehend. But this is not necessary: Menoeceus was deceiving his father when he was saying that he would go inside to bid Jocasta farewell, and any lingering to reveal his intention to Jocasta would detract from his urgent determination to go to the location where he will sacrifice himself. At 1090 the Messenger mentions Menoeceus' death as a prelude to and guarantee of the victorious battle of the Thebans against the Argives, and Jocasta's reaction to the narrative is not frigid but makes perfect sense, as she speaks of the mingled emotions it has caused, that is, joy to his country and grief to his father (1202-7).

Fourth episode (1067-283)

The Messenger enters in haste through the *parodos* which leads from the battlefield (possibly on the left), finds the palace shut and calls Jocasta. Because he is Eteocles' attendant he may have appeared before the audience earlier on as a silent extra accompanying Eteocles. At 1213, the Messenger's request to Jocasta to let him go implies physical activity with Jocasta possibly trying to block his exit.[27] Jocasta summons Antigone from the inside of the palace at 1264 and Antigone exits at 1270. This scene will be recalled when Antigone calls her father to come out of the palace in the exodos. Jocasta, Antigone and the Messenger as guide rush out through the *parodos* that leads to the battlefield

Exodos (1308-766)

Creon enters the stage, probably alone, as he does not yet function as the default ruler of Thebes and is absorbed in private grief.[28] The text at 1308 says that his brow is clouded by the news of his son's self-inflicted death, which may have also accompanied a change of Creon's mask before his appearance,[29] though this is not necessary, especially as in Creon's scene with Oedipus and Antigone he plays the role of the default ruler and not that of the bereaved father. When a second Messenger arrives, his words may be said to be addressed to the Chorus, but it is reasonable to think that Creon is still onstage, although keeping silent until 1584. Antigone enters, accompanied by silent extras, possibly dressed as soldiers, who bring the bodies of Jocasta, Eteocles and Polynices. The corpses may have been represented by dummies bearing the relevant masks of the characters and were probably placed prominently at the centre of the stage. The physical presence of the three bodies onstage, perhaps with Jocasta lying in the middle, is a strong and bitter visual reminder of the *agôn* scene where Jocasta arbitrated between her sons and also of their dying scene envisaged by the audience in the vivid narrative by the Messenger.

Antigone's singing part mirrors Jocasta's song upon meeting with Polynices. Antigone has changed from the bright clothes to clothes of mourning, a shift that may have taken place onstage by the actor shedding the saffron robe which was appropriate earlier and putting on some dark clothes handed over by an attendant. She sings, probably accompanying her song with dance movements, addresses Polynices, and leaves a lock of her hair on the biers. Her summoning of her father, and his subsequent exit from the palace, mirror the scene where Jocasta summoned Antigone to emerge from the house (1264-83). Oedipus' phraseology at 1539-40, referring to the support given to his steps, may have either an actual meaning (a staff as a stage-prop) or a metaphorical one (Antigone as her father's support). The spectators of the original performance could actually see whether Oedipus' reference was to a stage-prop or whether it was used as a metaphor. As Mastronarde[30] points out, it may be more plausible to think that Oedipus here means the staff he is carrying, as throughout their duet Oedipus ought to be able to stand on his own leaving Antigone free to make her own movements. The lyric exchange between father and daughter, where Oedipus is informed of the three deaths, is highly emotional in tone and effect. Creon is either present onstage from the beginning of the episode and throughout this exchange, or enters suddenly and unannounced at 1584 to make proclamations. Oedipus' reflection on his miserable life echoes Jocasta's opening account of the troubled past of the Labdacids.

In the exchange between Creon and Oedipus, Creon insists on his decision to exile Oedipus and then turns to the corpses, commanding that Eteocles' body should be taken inside and Polynices' body left unburied, and finally to Antigone, ordering her to withdraw in the house. At 1660 he commands his attendants to seize Antigone, which apparently they try to do. Antigone probably makes a gesture towards them to make sure that they do not hinder her from touching Polynices' body. At 1677, Antigone's oath 'by the sword' that she will kill Haemon if Creon insists on their marriage is either a reference to an imaginary sword by which each Danaid of the famous myth killed her husband on the wedding-night, or possibly a clue to Antigone grasping a sword from the corpses. It is true that there is no demonstrative pronoun accompanying the word 'sword' to make sure that Antigone refers to a prop, but the actual staging of Antigone grasping a sword would be stronger in terms of dramatic impact. At 1665 she begs Creon by her mother, probably gesturing towards Jocasta's corpse, and at 1671 she kisses Polynices' lips. After Antigone's display of defiance Creon probably leaves the stage at 1682 (rather than staying silently till the end of the play), either through the *parodos* leading to his house or probably through the central door of the palace to suggest his new role of ruler of Thebes. Oedipus asks Antigone's help at 1693 to reach the corpses. There follows an emotional scene where Antigone directs her father's hand towards the bodies. He touches Jocasta at 1695, whom he pathetically calls 'mother and wife', and asks for his sons; Antigone places his hand on their faces at 1700.

The scene ends with Oedipus announcing their destination, Colonus in Attica, and asking Antigone to be his guide. She takes his hand at 1710, guiding his steps (cf. Sophocles' *Oedipus at Colonus* 188-201) as they slowly move out of the acting area. Antigone's use of the adverb 'here' four times (1720-1) as she shows the way to her father has been taken[31] as a reference to the four steps that separate the stage from the *orchêstra*, echoing a similar reference by Tiresias when he moved from the *orchêstra* into the stage, although this cannot be certain.[32] Oedipus' first-person request to the Theban citizens 'look, here is Oedipus' (1758-61) recalls Sophocles' *Oedipus the King* 1524ff., where the Chorus invite the Thebans to see Oedipus. The words of the Euripidean Oedipus here, addressed to the Chorus who, however, are foreigners and not

'Theban citizens', have been suspected for interpolation.[33] More specifically, Oedipus' final words also imply an actor's self-conscious address to the audience to see him, who has played the role of Oedipus.[34] Eventually, the Chorus are left in the *orchêstra* while the three corpses and the attendants are still onstage. Alternatively, the corpses, which are still on stage at 1702, may be carried off stage as Antigone and her father start departing at 1709.

*

To conclude, the play is rich in terms of staging and performance. A careful evaluation of their contribution to the interpretation of the play shows that they greatly illuminate various dramatic concerns, guiding their reception by the audience, as well as establishing links between different scenes, which mirror one another, stressing their similarities or revealing their contrasts. This contribution is especially necessary due to the great length of the play, whereby visual effect may be said to carry an added impact on the audience's minds.

6

Reception

The myth of the fratricidal conflict between Eteocles and Polynices has received numerous treatments, both in literature and in the arts, throughout the centuries.[1] Since it explores issues such as the ardent wish for absolute power and the disastrous consequences of strife, it acquires added relevance, hence greater popularity, at times of political crisis involving tyrannical regimes or civil war. The history of the reception of the myth is vast and needs to be distinguished from the history of the reception of the play, which is the focus of the present chapter, as later treatments often go back not to Euripides but to Roman poets, especially Seneca and Statius. To mention one example, the myth is adapted in several romances in the Middle Ages, but these are informed especially by Statius.[2] The following discussion will start with an examination of the popularity of the play in antiquity and will then offer a close analysis of two influential Roman adaptations in tragedy and epic, namely by Seneca and Statius. The last section will examine the performance history of the play from the Renaissance to the present day.

The popularity of the play in antiquity

Suspected lines in the text of *Phoenician Women*, which are often regarded as actors' interpolations, imply stage revivals of the play in antiquity, although epigraphic evidence is admittedly silent on the issue.[3] The rich pictorial record from the late third century (see below) may also be said to refer to revivals of the play in subsequent times. The popularity[4] of the play in antiquity is evident in the numerous papyri, which surpass in number every other tragic text and attest its large dissemination, in the comic parodies as well as in the numerous quotations in other works, which give the play a rich list of testimonia (evidence for indirect tradition of the play).[5] Aristophanes composed a comedy with the title *Phoenician Women*, a fragment (fr. 570 K-A) of which is quoted by Athenaeus (4.154 E) and seems to be a parody of lines 1354-5 from Euripides' play, where Creon asks the Messenger how the brothers' mutual slaughter took place.[6] Lines 1595-9 (the beginning of Oedipus' *excursus* on his miseries) were parodied by Aristophanes in *Frogs* 1185-6, and lines 460-1 were parodied by Strattis, a comic playwright of the fifth century who wrote 'paratragic' comedies, in his comedy, also entitled *Phoenician Women* (Athenaeus 160b), where he quotes l.460 (Jocasta's 'I want to give you both some sensible advice') followed by 'when you boil lentils don't pour on perfume'.[7]

Diodorus of Sicily records an anecdote that shows the popularity of Euripides' *Phoenician Women* and its use as a parallel to historical events at Athens a few years after its original performance.[8] According to Diodorus (13.97.6), just before the sea-battle between Athens and Sparta off Arginusae in 406, the Athenian admiral Thrasybulus saw in his dream that he together with his six fellow-admirals were actors in the theatre playing the roles of the Seven against Thebes in Euripides' *Phoenician Women*. He also saw opposite them the enemy leaders from Euripides' *Suppliants*, and he was said to have interpreted his dream as a sign that the Athenians would prevail in the naval confrontation, but only just barely.

The note of the second hypothesis that the play is 'full of many fine sayings (*gnômôn*)', and also Thomas Magister's remark about the beautiful and multi-coloured *gnômai* of the play,[9] relate to an aspect of the play's content which must have caused it to be very frequently quoted in later authors and to feature prominently in the gnomological tradition of subsequent times. *Gnômai* ('fine sayings' or 'maxims') constituted an important part of education; the grammarian would ask the pupils to write down and memorize them, then make their own collections, and at a later stage the teacher of rhetoric would teach his pupils how to use them most effectively in compositions of their own.[10] The rich gnomic material of the play as well as the use of the myth of the Labdacids must have contributed to the choice of the *Phoenician Women* for educational purposes. In Byzantine times too, two gnomological corpora[11] cite verses from the play, including the Tutor's 'misogynistic' comments at the end of the Teichoskopia scene and the openings of Eteocles' and Polynices' speeches in the debate. Another aspect of the play which had a lasting appeal was its rhetoric, and there is evidence that the debate between Eteocles and Polynices, in particular, became a subject for rhetorical exercise at schools in the 3rd century AD.[12]

Quotations on themes like the love for one's country, the misery of exile or parental love for children feature in Plutarch's *Morals* and in Stobaeus' *Anthology*, while the theme of exile in particular was used by philosophers, like the Cynic Teles and the Stoic Musonius, who attacked the conventional view that separation from one's homeland amounts to misery and thus used Polynices as a negative example.[13] The evils of *pleonexia*, 'greed' and the praise of equality as formulated by Euripides' Jocasta attracted the interest of both Dio Chrysostom (17.6-17.7), who quotes her words in his own discussion of *pleonexia*, and of his contemporary Plutarch, whose *Life of Pyrrhus* not merely includes quotations from the Euripidean play but seems to be informed by it, especially in terms of the juxtaposition between *pleonexia* on the one hand and equality and friendship on the other, as well as in terms of the futility of extreme ambition.[14] As royal succession and ambitious monarchy were issues with added significance during the time of Dio Chrysostom, Plutarch and their readers (1st-2nd century AD), the thematic concerns of Euripides' *Phoenician Women* may have aroused a further interest in this context.

Aristotle mentions the Euripidean play as an example of the discord caused when each claims rule for himself in his *Nicomachean Ethics* (9.6.2). Eteocles' statement at 524-5 that 'if one is to do wrong, then it is finest to do wrong for the sake of monarchy; in other respects one should act justly' was reported by Cicero (*On Duties* 3.21.82) as a favourite of Julius Caesar's. Caesar said this as he was preparing to vanquish Pompey and seize power. In his epic *Pharsalia* or *Civil War*, Lucan writes about the confrontation between these two men, which was regarded as war between kin, since Caesar and Pompey were related by marriage. In this context, the fratricidal conflict of the *Phoenician Women* seems to have acquired a further relevance. Cicero also used line 506 ('to possess Monarchy, the greatest of gods'), spoken by Eteocles, to condemn Caesar's longing for absolute power. Suetonius (*Life of Augustus*, 25) also reports that Augustus was fond of quoting l. 599: 'the prudent general is better than the audacious one'.

Quotations from the *Phoenician Women* in association with Roman emperors occur in two other instances:[15] Firstly, Dio Cassius reports (58.24) an anecdote that a poet during Tiberius' reign (AD 14-37) named Aemilius Scaurus, had a character in his tragedy *Atreus* who suffered under Atreus' rule complain and receive the warning to keep quiet, for one would rather tolerate a tyrant's stupidities. As Dio mentions, Scaurus had in mind the verse 'One has to endure the stupidities of those who rule' from Euripides' *Phoenician Women* (393). According to the anecdote, when Tiberius heard this he said that if Scaurus made him Atreus he would make him Ajax in turn, and as a result the tragic poet was forced to commit suicide. The anecdote refers to Mamercus Aemilius Scaurus, a distinguished orator and poet who committed suicide in AD 34, after causing Tiberius' displeasure when his tragedy was considered by his enemy Macro, the prefect of the Praetorian guard, to be offensive to Tiberius. Secondly, the emperor Julian in an essay against the Cynic Heraclius mentions the tragic curse over the sons along with line 68 from the *Phoenician Women* ('that they should share this inheritance by the whetted sword').

The Menoeceus episode in particular, believed to be a

Euripidean invention, attracted a considerable amount of interest in subsequent times:[16] Cicero (*Tusculan Disputations* 1.48.116) mentions this self-sacrifice along with that of the daughters of Erechtheus and Iphigenia among the *topoi* used by orators on patriotic issues, and Statius in his epic *Thebaid* devotes a large section to this episode (10.650ff.). Philostratus in his *Images* (1.4) describes an image of Menoeceus' death, Pausanias writes that he saw his tomb in Thebes (9.25.1), though in his version it was Apollo's oracle that demanded the sacrifice, and Lucian in his treatise *On Dancing* (43) mentions Menoeceus' death as one of the subjects for the pantomimes performed in Roman time. This is interesting in view of the relative lack of prominence of the episode in the play.

With regard to iconography, post-Euripidean artistic presentations often depict the duel between the two brothers: it appears on Etruscan funerary urns, between the 4th and 2nd centuries BC, where the two brothers appear thrusting swords into each other's body simultaneously, as on an Etruscan sarcophagus in the Vatican.[17] An Etruscan ash-chest in Copenhagen depicts the two brothers urged by the Furies,[18] while a cup in Hall, dated to the late 3rd/early 2nd century BC, depicts the two brothers after their duel. Eteocles here is already dead and Polynices extends his hand toward Jocasta, who is committing suicide. Antigone is shown lamenting, while there are also two female figures personifying Argos on the left and Thebes on the right, as well as a female figure or figures called 'paternal', which may imply the personification of Oedipus' curse, which is called a Fury or Furies in the Euripidean play (624, 1306, 1503).[19]

A neck-amphora in London by the Ixion painter, dated in 330/10 BC depicts Antigone and the Tutor,[20] while a bowl in London (Fig. 1), dated to the end of the third/beginning of the second century BC, shows a series of scenes from the Euripidean play, with Eteocles and Polynices fighting while the personification of Thebes is watching their duel, and with Antigone and Creon each in two different scenes:[21] Antigone supplicates Creon, half-turned away from her, to allow her to bury the corpse of Polynices, and on the other side of the circular surface

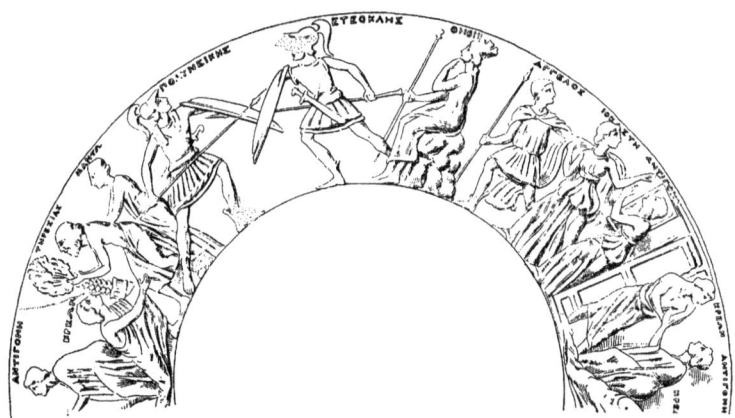

Fig. 1. Homeric bowl, dated to the end of the third/beginning of the second century BC, depicting scenes from Euripides' *Phoenician Women*. British Museum, London, G 104 (*Lexicon Iconographicum Mythologiae Classicae*, vol. 1.1, s.v. 'Antigone', nos 6 and 9).

Creon clasps Tiresias' knees with both hands.[22] Tiresias' daughter, Manto, is standing behind her father. The same bowl also depicts Jocasta, Antigone and the Messenger hastening to the battlefield,[23] while some Etruscan vase paintings, dated to the 2nd century BC, depict Jocasta and Antigone trying to restrain the two brothers who prepare to fight each other.[24] A bowl at Halle University, dated to the second century BC,[25] depicts the scene with Jocasta and Antigone over the bodies of the two brothers. Oedipus' request to Antigone to lead him to the bodies of Jocasta and his sons is illustrated on another bowl,[26] dated to the second century BC, depicting a bent old man with his hands stretched towards the ground and bearing a caption paraphrasing Oedipus' lines. The existence of such captions, which represent the direct evidence of the artists' familiarity with literary works, reflects in general the increasing literacy in the Hellenistic period. Finally, the scene with Oedipus among the corpses of his sons featured in Etruscan painting during the second and the first centuries BC.[27]

Roman adaptations

The tragic poets of the Republican Rome often modelled their tragedies on earlier Greek plays. Livius Accius composed a tragedy with the title *Phoenissae*, from which only a few verses survive.[28] The first four verses indicate a knowledge of the opening of the Euripidean play.[29] In Accius' version, which seems to omit Oedipus' curse, it is Oedipus himself who has ordained that his sons alternate in power (a variation on the myth found also in Hyginus, *Fabula* 67 and perhaps implied also in Seneca's *Phoenissae*), and he is alive during the conflict of his sons. At the end of the Roman play Creon exiles Oedipus and Antigone may follow her father.

Livius Annaeus Seneca composed his *Phoenissae* around AD 62, and this is regarded as his last tragedy.[30] The manuscript tradition preserves two titles for the play: *Phoenissae*, which recalls the Euripidean play, and the *Thebaid*, which is a more appropriate title for an epic than for a tragedy. A striking feature of the play is its lack of choral odes, which is one of the characteristics that have led critics to think that the play is incomplete. There are changes in the setting: at the opening of the drama the setting is the rough terrain outside the city of Thebes, at 363 it becomes the walls of Thebes and at 443 it turns into the battlefield. With regard, in particular, to the scene with Antigone, Jocasta and the Attendant (363-442), where the setting changes to the battlements (or the palace roof), Seneca may have been influenced by the Euripidean Teichoskopia scene. The dramatic time is three years after Eteocles came to the throne following his father's abdication. Seneca follows the Euripidean version, which keeps Jocasta alive after the revelation of the crimes and willing to avert the fighting of the brothers.[31] Oedipus is not imprisoned by his sons as in Euripides, but has abdicated the throne willingly and left Thebes, now accompanied by Antigone in his wandering. Contrary to the Euripidean play, which focuses on the fraternal strife, the Senecan play focuses on the reactions to the conflict by the brothers' parents. In the figures of Oedipus and Jocasta,

Seneca juxtaposes the disastrous effects of passion and the positive effects of reason, while in the figures of their sons Seneca exploits themes familiar elsewhere in his plays, that is, the lust to rule, passion and the corruption of absolute political power.

There are two main sections, the first focusing on the character of Oedipus and the second on the figure of Jocasta, recalling Sophocles' *Oedipus at Colonus* and Euripides' *Phoenician Women* respectively. Both characters are asked by Antigone and an outsider (a Messenger and an Attendant) to intervene between their sons, and the play dramatizes their opposite reactions. Oedipus does not wish to mediate, stresses his sons' lack of piety and even wishes that they commit fratricide. He is presented as filled with anger, self-hatred and hatred for others, while his roaming outside Thebes in the wild seems to have made him savage. He is very different from his Euripidean counterpart, who may have cursed his sons, but seemed to have repented of it. He perhaps owes more to the wrathful Oedipus of Sophocles' *Oedipus at Colonus* with regard to his attitude to his sons, though the Senecan version further intensifies Oedipus' anger. Jocasta, by contrast, is willing to attempt to put an end to the fraternal strife and Seneca heightens the tension by having her rush to the battlefield and place herself between the enemy armies.

The abundance of terms which refer to consanguinity and the substitution of family terms for proper names are distinctive features of the play, which highlight the genetic chaos of the incestuous royal family of Thebes.[32] Seneca lays great emphasis on the notion of guilt, and although he too, like Euripides before, mentions Oedipus' ignorance and innocence, nevertheless his Oedipus cannot overcome his feeling of guilt and wishes that his sons surpass their father in sin (335-6). Seneca, like Accius, does not use Oedipus' curse on his sons as the source of their conflict but points out their tainted origins as the ultimate source of their crimes, as their incestuous descent entraps them in a cycle where crimes are repeated (335-6, 368-9). As Oedipus remarks in his ominous prophecy of the fated future woes, no-one will hold the royal sceptre without accursed blood, as the seeds of future catastrophe are already sown (277-80, cf. 648-9). But although

Seneca stresses the fate affecting the brothers, he shows, like Euripides, that they have personal responsibility, as the decision on whether to fight each other is a matter of choice (453-5). According to Jocasta, although both brothers can do nothing to alter their doomed heritage, they can at least freely decide on desisting from war. Oedipus' anger (352) which dictates his actions is well summarized in his phrase 'let the entire house collapse to its foundations, let the city be cremated (345-6),[33] and is matched by his sons' raging fury (290, 302) and anger (299). For an audience who have been influenced by Stoic philosophy, both Oedipus and his sons are examples of the disastrous predominance of passion over reason.

Antigone, who undergoes a change from a secluded maiden to a defiant figure in Euripides, is presented by Seneca as a dominant figure, who rationally converses with her father and tries to dissuade him from committing suicide by urging him to endure misfortune with courage, echoing the Stoics in advocating a rationalistic approach to life, including the triumph of reason over mad desire for death.[34] She urges her mother to actively mediate by placing herself between the armies. Her request to her mother to place her bared breast between her sons' swords (405) may have been inspired by the Euripidean references to Jocasta's breasts as symbols of her motherhood, while Jocasta's reported tears and entreaties to her sons (440-2) recall the Euripidean Jocasta's frustrated attempt to reach her sons on the battlefield and to use any kind of entreaty in order to dissuade them from fighting each other.[35] The Senecan Polynices receives a relatively favourable portrayal reminiscent of his Euripidean counterpart, and Seneca too gives emphasis to the misery of exile, while Eteocles recalls the Euripidean character through his insatiable lust for power. In particular, his phrase 'power is well bought at any price' (664), with which the play ends, echoes the Euripidean Eteocles' 'If one is to do wrong, then it is finest to do wrong for the sake of monarchy; in other respects one should act justly' (524-5). Seneca also dramatizes Polynices' fear and distrust even of his mother (478-80), insists on his need for wealth and his fear of poverty (595-8) and has Jocasta lament the fact that she did not attend to her son's wedding (505-10) as well as ask her son how he will allow himself to destroy his homeland (565-82). These passages all recall the arguments used by the Euripidean Jocasta in her address to Polynices.

The series of Roman civil wars during the first century BC seems to have left an impact on the epics as well as the tragedies of the first century AD. If Lucan's *Pharsalia* treated the war between Caesar and Pompey as war between kin, Publius Papinius Statius turned to the fraternal conflict between Eteocles and Polynices in his *Thebaid* (AD 92) in twelve books. Written in hexameters, it treats the same subject as the (fragmentary) Greek epic *Thebaid*, of Antimachus of Colophon (*c*. 410 BC), which also treated the Argive expedition against Thebes and may have been familiar to Statius. Antimachus was a model for the learned Alexandrian scholars and the emperor Hadrian considered him superior to Homer. But Statius' main source for his epic is Euripides' *Phoenician Women*.[36] Statius focuses on the fraternal strife between Eteocles and Polynices and poignantly retards their final confrontation for a greater effect. His strong emphasis on characterization shows how egotism and impiety generate conflict and foreshadow catastrophe. The first six books treat the events that lead up to the war and the last six treat the war and its aftermath.

Book 7 includes a section (243-373) which gives a survey of the army, reminiscent of the Euripidean Teichoskopia scene. In Statius, Antigone stands on a tower and learns from an old-man, Laius' onetime armour-bearer, about the troops and their leaders. Book 7 (470-527) also includes Jocasta's intervention, but in the epic she rushes to the Argive camp along with Antigone and Ismene and pleads only with Polynices. Polynices' emotional address to his mother and his embraces of her and his two sisters are followed by a series of questions (497-504) by Jocasta, bringing to the fore her bitterness at her son's feigned tears and gestures, which aim at stirring compassion, whereas in reality her son is now nothing but an Argive enemy. This bitter reaction to what Jocasta perceives as her son's feigned attitude is not found in Euripides, though there too Polynices' emotional behaviour upon entering the city and seeing his mother could be interpreted as deliberately aimed at eliciting her sympathy (see Chapter 5). In Statius Jocasta invites Polynices to meet with his brother and let her judge their claims to the throne (508-9) and asks him not to be suspicious of either Eteocles or herself. The role of Jocasta as the arbiter as well as the notion that Polynices distrusts both his brother and his own mother are elements previously employed by Euripides. Statius raises these issues and makes both the army (527-9) and Polynices softened by Jocasta's words. Polynices kisses his mother and his sisters and the narrator interprets his emotional outburst as an indication that at that moment 'the throne was forgotten' (537). What Statius does is to shift the emphasis to Tydeus, who utters a speech (539-59) against Jocasta and in favour of the continuation of the war, which leads to Jocasta's exit from the camp with her daughters (609-11).

A long section is devoted to Antigone and Ismene in an inner chamber conversing about not simply the present woes but also the ill-fated past of their family (8.607-36). This linking of the troubled present with the doomed past is a judicious evaluation of the situation here expressed by the two sisters, the 'innocent children of unhappy Oedipus' (608-9). Their balanced approach here recalls that of the Euripidean Jocasta's. Their shifting sympathies from Eteocles to Polynices mark the problematic situation at hand as one laments Eteocles, the other laments Polynices and both lament the war (612-13).

Fear and the desire for self-preservation make the people dissociate themselves from their king's cause, express the wish that he should give a share of the throne to his brother and beg Tiresias for a prophecy (584-91). Statius here elaborates a situation which may have been an inspired response to the Euripidean account, by exploiting the gap between what Eteocles on the one hand, and the people of Thebes on the other, fight for. Whereas Eteocles (in both Euripides and Statius) defends his people against the Argive attack, his ultimate motive is not defence of his people, but his egotistical clinging to the throne in his personal clash with his brother at the expense of the safety of his city. The mention of Tiresias leads to a section which is strongly reminiscent of the Euripidean play: Tiresias' oracle that Theban victory will be secured by the sacrifice of the youngest of the race of the serpent to appease the snake of Mars (Roman Ares) (610-15), Creon's fear for his son's life and his supplication of the prophet (616-26) and Menoeceus' sacrifice, which dominates the rest of book 10. The sacrifice of Menoeceus in Statius' account acquires a strong public character as the oracle is asked for by the people and then spread from mouth to mouth (626-7), and it is the people too who rejoice at the future sacrifice of Menoeceus; they hail him as saviour (683-5) and later escort his body in acts of reverence and honour (783-90).

The episode of Menoeceus is filled with a notion of grandeur which greatly enhances both the notion of the nobility of Menoeceus' patriotic self-sacrifice and the importance of its effect for the salvation of the city. Both Menoeceus' self-abnegation and the association of his sacrifice with the salvation of the city were treated by Euripides, but because his main concern was with the fratricidal strife, the emphasis moved away from Menoeceus to the fate of the brothers. By contrast, Statius clearly stresses the public appreciation of this sacrifice as the means of saving the city, before moving to the treatment of the fight between the two brothers in book 11. In a majestic description of divine visitation of a mortal (10.632-81), Valour is said to find Menoeceus while he is fighting on the battlefield and overwhelm him by supernatural power, which overcomes his initial hesitation and prompts him to the noble destiny that awaits him. The Euripidean scene between Creon and Menoeceus, where the son cheats his father into believing that he will not sacrifice himself, is elaborated at this part of the narrative by Statius (686-735), where his Menoeceus turns his father's fear aside by also playing a trick on him: he pretends that his brother Haemon has been wounded and that he intends to go and bring a doctor to tend to his wounds. The account of his admirable self-sacrifice is followed by the narrator's remark that his body was carried by Piety and Valour and that his spirit is next to Jupiter (780-2), and closes with the honours given to him by the Thebans (783-90). Thus, Menoeceus' sacrifice is structurally framed and significantly elevated by both public approval and divine involvement.

Further, the Euripidean juxtaposition between the selfless act of Menoeceus and the egotistical lust of the brothers is given a stark emphasis by Statius, when he has Menoeceus' mother (792-814) burst out in tears and complain that while she laments her son who was the product of no incestuous union, Jocasta has her children, and that her son has perished so that Eteocles and Polynices may take turns on the throne. The sacrifice of Menoeceus informs the angry exchange betwen Creon and Eteocles in book 11 (262-314), where Creon, filled with rage and grief at his son's death, reprimands Eteocles for his delay only to cause Eteocles to accuse him of taking advantage of his son's glorious death in order to promote his ambition to succeed to the vacant throne of Thebes. Statius shows Jocasta intervening once again, this time to plead with Eteocles in vain (315-53).

Book 11 describes the duel between the brothers; here, contrary to Euripides, where the proposal for a duel comes from Eteocles, Statius has (11.168-9) Polynices make this proposal. The impropriety of the fratricidal strife is here shown not only by Adrastus' intervention (424-35) but also by references to Valour and Piety, which make a sharp contrast to their role in the Menoeceus episode. The fratricidal lust makes Valour vanish (412) and Piety is said to have withdrawn from earth lamenting and trying in vain to prevent slaughter (457-70). Although Statius gives emphasis to the overall divine framework surrounding the mortal clash and shows how in the end the Furies rejoice at the upcoming deaths, the narrator's remark that Furies are no longer needed, as human madness surpasses them (537-8) highlights the notion that human motivation is more powerful than any divine intervention. Euripides too dramatized the double effects of divine motivation (curse and the gods' ambiguous involvement) and human motivation and suggested that human responsibility acquired the greatest role in the development of the events. Statius accentuates this process by unmasking the brothers' fratricidal lust as a kind of madness which needs no divine catalyst. The actual description of the duel recalls the one in Euripides, as here too a brother (Eteocles in Euripides, Polynices in Statius) hastens to announce himself the victor only to be killed in turn (552-73), though Statius leaves no room for a reconciliation at the moment of death and implies that the bitter hatred between the two brothers will continue even after death.

Finally, Statius makes Jocasta kill herself with Laius' sword, which Oedipus had taken as a spoil (11.634-7), has Creon take the sceptre (650-1), and elaborates a scene where Oedipus asks Antigone, who assists him, to lead him to the corpses of his sons (586-95), as well as a longer scene (669-756) with an intense verbal clash between Creon and Oedipus, with Antigone in a pleading role, which ends in Creon's not banishing Oedipus from Thebes but ordering him to confine himself in the wilds outside the city (cf. the setting at the beginning of Seneca's *Phoenissae*).

From the Renaissance to the present

From the sixteenth century onwards, Euripides' *Phoenician Women* became widely known from the Latin translations[37] by Stiblinus (1562) and Grotius (1630) and was one of the most admired tragedies in both the 16th and 17th centuries. This appeal reflects this period's aesthetics, which showed a great appreciation of the high degree of emotion, of rhetoric, of the multiplicity of dramatic action (with the proliferation of events and the inclusion of sub-plots), and of the nobility of diction and sentiment as enhancing the power of the tragic genre. All these characteristics, which recall the remarks made in the second ancient hypothesis to the play as well as the remark by Quintilian (*The Orator's Education* 10.1.67-8) that Euripides' *sententiae* and treatment of emotions made him a superb trage-dian, are interestingly reflected in the prefaces to the translations by Stiblinus and especially by Grotius and show the interest of this period in tragedy as a genre of elevated diction and morality.[38]

An early adaptation of Euripides' *Phoenician Women* was George Gascoigne's *Jocasta*, performed at Gray's Inn in 1566.[39] The first and fourth acts were written by Francis Kinwelmersh, the second, third and fifth by George Gascoigne, while Christopher Yelverton wrote the epilogue. Gascoigne was probably in charge of the entire project, as he later included the play in his collected works. Each act was preceded by a dumb-show with music. Gascoigne and Kinwelmersh did not use the Euripidean original as they claimed, but used instead an Italian adaptation of the Euripidean tragedy by Lodovico Dolce (1508-68), entitled *Giocasta* (1549). Dolce had translated Seneca's tragedies and other Latin texts but had a limited knowledge of ancient Greek. For his own translation he relied on the Latin translation of Euripides' *Phoenician Women* published by R. Winter in 1541. Dolce's work is a free translation of the original, where he omits scenes and adds others, making ample use of Seneca.

Elements from both the Euripidean and the Senecan reconciliation scenes appeared in an Italian comedy by Giambattista Della Porta, entitled *Gli duoi fratelli rivali* ('The two rival brothers'), in 1601 in Thomas Goffe's *The Courageous Turk* in 1618. The latter work, which treated the conflict between the Turks and the Serbs on Kosovo field in 1384 as symbolical of that between Mohammendism and Christianity, has been characterized as a Jacobean 'Phoenician Women'.[40]

Jean Baptiste Racine adapted Euripides' *Phoenician Women* in *La Thébaïde, ou, les Frères Ennemis: Étéocle et Polynice* ('The Thebaid, or, the enemy brothers: Eteocles and Polynices') in 1664.[41] This was the first tragedy by Racine, generally considered to be the greatest writer of French classical tragedy and one of the most famous French writers of his time along with Molière and Corneille. The play was performed at the Palais-Royal by Molière's company. Unlike most of the dramatists of his era, Racine had a thorough training in Classics and was able to read the Greek tragedians in the original Greek. In the preface to his play Racine states that he regards the fate of Oedipus' sons as the most tragic subject,[42] and notes that Euripides' *Phoenician Women* has been his exemplar.[43] In Racine too Jocaste (Jocasta) opens the tragedy and expresses her anxiety over the impending duel, the two brothers meet (though Racine retards their meeting until Act IV, scene III, where Polynice's (Polynices) motivation is explored in further detail than in Euripides.[44] They end feeling more hatred for each other, decide, not on the battlefield but before their mother, to settle the strife by means of a duel (first proposed, as in Statius, by Polynice) and an oracle demands the sacrifice of Ménécée (Menoeceus), who resigns himself to his fate. His sacrifice is in fact used as a pretext by Étéocle (Eteocles) to continue the war in order to avenge the death of his cousin. Jocaste is a wise character who tries to avert fratricide, but she is overcome with despair and gives up the attempt earlier than her Euripidean counterpart: she commits suicide before her sons kill each other when she realizes that they have failed to be reconciled.

In 1723, an adaptation was made by Jane Robe of both Euripides' *Phoenician Women* and Racine's *La Thébaïde*, entitled *The Fatal Legacy* and performed on 23 April 1723 at Lincoln's Inn Fields, London. The myth of the fratricidal strife must have seemed particularly appealing, as the historical context of this production followed the period when Great Britain was torn by civil war (17th century) and Jacobite uprisings (18th century); the Jacobite invasion occurred a few years earlier, in 1715, and the play echoed an anti-Jacobite cause especially in the presentation of Polynices as an autocratic pretender.[45] The Jacobite invasion of 1745 is reflected in William Mason's drama entitled *Elfrida*. This play, performed on 21 November 1772 at Covent Garden, London, bears a strong anti-despotical tone and attacks the invaders, echoing Euripides' *Phoenician Women* along with other Greek tragedies.[46]

During the nineteenth century several other works treated the subject of the fraternal strife, in ways which ranged from direct imitation to remote adaptation. Friedrich Schiller, whose works include a translation of Euripides' *Phoenician Women*, wrote the tragedy *Die Braut von Messina* ('The Bride of Messina'), which premiered on 19 March 1803 in Weimar. The central theme of the drama is the fraternal conflict between the princes of Messina, Don Manuel and Don Caesar, following the death of their father, and the mediation of their mother, queen Isabella, to avert mutual carnage. When in their meeting before their mother at the beginning of the play the queen sees no hope for reconciliation, she significantly likens her sons to the 'Theban pair' who folded each other in a last embrace, thus clearly drawing a parallel between the present fratricidal strife and its archetype, that of Eteocles and Polynices.

The outbreak of the Greek War for Independence in 1821 led to a revived interest in Greek myth and tragedy in the 1820s, evident both in the Fine Arts (e.g. the painting by Francesco Podesti, depicting Eteocles and Polynices, in 1824) and especially in the performances of Greek tragedies. Edward Fitzball's *Antigone*, subtitled *The Theban Sister*, was a British adaptation based on Sophocles' *Antigone* and Euripides' *Phoenician Women* and first produced in Norwich Theatre Royal in 1821.[47] A British adaptation of the *Phoenician Women* appeared in the same year under the title *Ion*.[48] Written by the lawyer and politician Thomas Noon Talfourd, this five-act tragedy was based on Euripides' *Hippolytus*, *Ion*, *Phoenician Women* and Sophocles' *Antigone*, *Oedipus the King*, *Oedipus at Colonus* and *Trachiniae*. It treated the patriotic self-sacrifice of Ion, king of Argos, in response to the Delphic oracle which declared that the pestilence caused through the deeds of the royal family would only be removed through its extinction. It is not only from pestilence but also from tyranny that Ion frees his people as he announces constitutional reforms against monarchy and in favour of all classes. The play thus echoes the political situation of its era.

In Greece, Euripides' *Phoenician Women* has been performed several times since 1904.[49] In most cases the productions travel

6. Reception

widely around Greece and in modern times the proliferation of festivals has facilitated the spread of performances of ancient tragedies and the deep interest shown by the spectators, who regard the plays as a significant part of their cultural heritage. A performance of the play, directed by Linos Karzis in Athens in 1941, aroused the spirit of resistance among the school audience, as the young people reacted enthusiastically to the patriotic elements of the play, disregarding the German occupation forces which were present in the theatre. Linos Karzis and Alexis Minotis are two directors who worked on the play several times during their career. In 1960 the National Theatre of Greece, with Alexis Minotis as director, staged the *Phoenician Women* at the ancient theatre of Epidaurus. The music was composed by Mikis Theodorakis and the cast included famous Greek actors, such as Alexis Minotis as Oedipus, Katina Paxinou as Jocasta and the young Anna Synodinou as Antigone. On 27 March 1962, the 'international day for theatre', the National Theatre was given the special honour to open, with the performance of the *Phoenician Women*, the International Festival 'Théâtre des Nations' in Paris. Along with the performance of Aristophanes' *Birds* by the Greek Art Theatre, the National Theatre's *Phoenician Women* gave Greece the prize for the best national participation.

Modern Greek audiences may of course have recognized in the play echoes of their own predicaments, due, say, to the civil war in late 1940s or to the political turmoil because of the junta regime (1967-74), in the same way that in other cultures from antiquity onwards (e.g. Roman period, England in the 17th century) periods of civil strife seem to have enhanced the interest in the Euripidean play, given that fratricidal conflict is the main theme. The play also generated lyrical responses on the modern Greek stage. Mikis Theodorakis worked on the Euripidean play for his opera entitled *Antigone*, performed by the National Lyric Stage/State Orchestra of Athens, Greece, which premiered at the Athens Concert Hall (*Megaron Mousikês*) on 7 October 1999.[50] This lyrical adaptation was based on Aeschylus' *Seven against Thebes*, Euripides'

121

Phoenician Women and Sophocles' *Antigone* and *Oedipus the King*. It was directed by Vassilis Nikolaidis, with Mikis Theodorakis as both composer and librettist. Act 1, scene 2 includes the dialogue between Jocasta and Polynices, followed by Eteocles' entrance and his debate with his brother, the duel between the two brothers in front of their mother, their mutual deaths and Jocasta's suicide, while scene 3 shows Antigone's lament and clash with Creon. Overall, the adaptation of the Theban tragedies represented for Theodorakis the repeated drama that haunts the human race like a primordial curse, namely, war as the consequence of the thirst for power and domination.[51] Mikis Theodorakis' Symphony No 4, which premiered with the Athens Symphonic Orchestra on 3 May

Fig. 2. Jocasta (Antigone Valakou) with Eteocles (Dimitris Lignadis) on her right and Polynices (Konstantinos Markoulakis) on her left. Photograph from the rehearsal of the stage performance of Euripides' *Phoenician Women* by the State Theatre of Northern Greece in 1999 (directed by N. Chourmouziades). Photo: L. Tektonidis. Reproduced by courtesy of the Archive of the State Theatre of Northern Greece.

1987 in Athens, is another lyrical response to the Theban myth by the great Greek composer, based on Euripides' *Phoenician Women* along with Aeschylus' *Eumenides*, and focusing on human fate.[52]

Apart from Greece (Fig. 2), where performances of tragedy have a strong tradition, a mere survey of the production history of the *Phoenician Women* shows a remarkable geographical spread: Great Britain, USA, Italy, Germany, the Netherlands and Cyprus are only a few examples of the interest this play has generated. A few examples suffice to show that directorial interest is often attracted by the political resonances of the play, which is used to reflect contemporary concerns. In Germany the play (*Phoenizierinnen*, 'The Phoenician Women') was adapted by J. Berg and directed by Hansgünther Heyme in 1981 in a way which echoed contemporary preoccupations, as in this production, which was performed in Stuttgart, the Thebes-in-crisis depicted in the play became a symbol for the divided Berlin of that time.[53] A British production, directed by Katie Mitchell and staged by the Royal Shakespeare Company at Stratford upon Avon and London in 1995-6, had as a distinctive feature the adoption of Serbo-Croat chants in the performance of choral lyric. This use clearly shows how the troubled Balkans of the late twentieth century became a telling setting for performances of Greek tragedy.[54] Contemporary politics was also reflected in another British version, entitled *Thebans*. This play, which was directed by Graham McLaren and staged in 2003 in Edinburgh by Theatre Babel, was a liberal adaptation by Liz Lochhead, considered to be Scotland's greatest living dramatist, based on Euripides' *Phoenician Women*, Aeschylus' *Seven against Thebes* and Sophocles' Theban plays.[55] It echoed the contemporary clash between the West and the Arab world, which was evident especially in the Arabic-style military costume and headdress of Polynices as well as in the use of a photo of Saddam Hussein at the beginning. An American production with obvious political resonances was the adaptation entitled *The Phoenician Women*, and directed by David Travis, which was staged by Synapse Productions in New York in 2002. The Chorus here evoked the contemporary Middle East as they sang songs based on Arabic melodies and performed Semitic folk dances.[56]

Notes

1. Poet and Play

1. Collard 1981 gives a concise account of Euripides with further bibliography. See more recently Gregory 2005b. For brief accounts, see the introductions on the Aris & Phillips series (by S. Barlow) and in the 'Oxford World's Classics' series (by E. Hall), both with bibliography.

2. Lefkowitz 1981, 103, challenges the story of Euripides' death in Macedon, but maybe this is oversceptical.

3. See Kovacs 1994 for the ancient testimonia concerning Euripides' life and career.

4. See Lefkowitz 1981, 88-104, 163-9.

5. See Webster 1967, 21-30.

6. On Euripides and the sophists, see Conacher 1998; Allan 2000. On the sophists in general, see Guthrie 1971; Kerferd 1981; Wallace 1998. On the intellectual context, see Goldhill 1986, 222-43.

7. For Euripides' plays that are now either lost or in fragmentary form, see Webster 1967; Collard, Cropp and Lee 1995; Collard, Cropp and Gibert 2004; Cropp 2005, 280-6.

8. On Euripides' reception by his contemporaries, see Stevens 1976.

9. For a brief account of Euripides' reception since antiquity, see Gregory 2005b, 252-6.

10. On Euripides' use of myth, see esp. Eisner 1979. On the relation between Euripides and Aeschylus, see esp. Aélion 1983.

11. For these terms, used by critics like Kitto, Grube and Conacher, see in brief Storey and Allan 2005, 138.

12. On comic elements in Euripides, see Gregory 2000.

13. On slaves in Euripides, see Synodinou 1977. On the sociological aspects of Greek tragedy, with emphasis on Euripides, see Hall 1997.

14. Cf. Longinus in his treatise *On the Sublime* (15.3).

15. See Diggle 1999.

16. On women in Euripides, see esp. Powell 1990; Rabinowitz 1993. For women in Greek tragedy in general, see esp. Foley 2001.

17. Euripides' use of rhetoric reflects the pervasiveness of rhetoric in his society. As Winnington-Ingram (1969, 136) notes, 'the rhetoric which pervades his [*sc.* Euripides'] theatre was not a personal idiosyncracy, but an addiction of the Athenian people'. On rhetoric in debates, see esp. Duchemin 1945; Collard 1975; Conacher 1981; Lloyd 1992; Dubischar 2001. On the use of rhetoric in Greek tragedy in general, see Buxton 1982; Bers 1994; Pelling 2005.

18. On the 'political' plays of Euripides, see esp. Zuntz 1955. On several aspects of politics in Euripidean tragedies, see Gregory 1991.

19. On *Trojan Women*, see Croally 1994.

20. See Hall 1989.

21. On Euripides and religion, see esp. Lefkowitz 1987; Mikalson 1981; Yunis 1988.

22. On the 'new music', see in brief Storey and Allan 2005, 148-51.

23. Cf. Baldock 1989, 70.

24. On medicine and Euripides, see more recently Kosak 2004.

25. Because of the length of 1308-766, Mastronarde 1994, 511 and n. 1, takes 1308-479 as a fifth episode, 1480-581 as the equivalent of a *stasimon*, and the rest as the *exodos*.

26. For the 'open' structure, see Mastronarde 1994, 3.

27. On the transmission of tragic texts, see the concise account by Kovacs 2005, with bibliography. On the textual tradition of the *Phoenician Women*, see Mastronarde and Bremer (1982).

28. See Craik 1988, 40-1; Mastronarde 1994, 11-14; Amiech 2004, 13-14.

29. The mention of these plays along with *Phoenician Women* does not necessarily mean that they were parts of the same trilogy. On the question of the companion plays of *Phoenician Women*, see Mastronarde 1994, 13-14; Amiech 2004, 14-16.

30. On the textual tradition of Euripides and the problem of interpolation, see in brief Craik 1988, 49-55 and Mastronarde 1994, 39-49; Amiech 2004, 74-81.

31. The standard work on histrionic interpolation is Page 1934.

32. On the process of the canon formation, see Easterling 1997b, esp. 213 and 225.

33. Cf. Mastronarde 1994, 49-50. On the editions of the *Phoenician Women* since the Aldine, see Amiech 2004, 105-7.

2. Myth and Intertextuality

1. For the use of myth in Greek tragedy, see in brief Anderson 2005.

2. Kristeva 1980, 36. Kristeva's work was originally published in the 1960s (cf. Kristeva 1969). For the history of the term and its applications, see Allen 2000.

3. For a brief overview of the use of the Theban myth in tragedy, see Baldry 1956. For collective material and discussion of the myths around Thebes, see Vian 1963; Gantz 1993, vol. 2, 467-530 and *LIMC* under the names of various persons involved in them. See also Mueller-Goldingen 1985, 14-36; Mastronarde 1994, 17-30.

4. For the treatment of the myth in Stesichorus see below.

5. Mastronarde 1994, 21.

6. For brief discussions, see Davies 1989.

7. Stesichorus, fr. 222b *PMGF*. On this poem, see Parsons 1977; Gostoli 1978; Thalmann 1982; March 1987, 126-7; Maingon 1989; Pavese 1997.

8. March 1987, 127-31. See Mastronarde 1994, 25.

9. Mueller-Goldingen 1985, 34-5, argues that the maxim in 86-7 reflects 204-8 of Stesichorus; Tiresias' advice to the sons in the past 878f parallels his role in Stesichorus; and Jocasta's determination to join her sons in death is parallel to the mother's wish to die before witnessing the final strife of her sons in Stesichorus. Mastronarde (1994, 26 n. 1) discusses these parallels and rightly expresses reservations, arguing that the first example is a maxim and the third involves two distinct *topoi*. But the general idea of a mother's interference between the sons is a motif that may have been suggested to Euripides for his own dramatic purposes.

10. On the date of Euripides' *Oedipus*, see Collard, Cropp and Gibert 2004, 112.

11. See Collard, Cropp and Gibert 2004, 107.

12. See Hutchinson 1985, 209-11.

13. Cf. Griffith 1999 on Sophocles' *Antigone* 1302-3. For the view that Menoeceus is a Euripidean variation on Megareus, see Vian 1963, 208-14 and Aélion 1983, vol. 1, 201-3.

14. On Menoeceus as a Euripidean invention, see Mastronarde 1994, 28-9.

15. See Bushnell 1988, esp. 111-14. Cf. Kamerbeek 1965, 39.

16. The reference to Tiresias' admonitions to Oedipus' sons in the past may also be an intertextual allusion to his similar role in Stesichorus (222b *PMGF*).

17. Mastronarde 1994, 22 and n. 3.

18. On this fragmentary play, see Collard, Cropp and Gibert 2004, 105-32.

19. Mastronarde 1994 on 62.

20. Mastronarde 1994, 23 and n. 1.

21. Mastronarde 1994 on 63 and n. 1.

22. Mueller-Goldingen 1985, 36.

23. See Mastronarde 1994, 23 n. 4.

24. See Hutchinson 1985, xxv.

25. See Hutchinson 1985, xxiv, xxix.

26. The question of the relative ages of Eteocles and Polynices varies. In *Phoenician Women* Eteocles is presented as the older brother whereas Sophocles makes Polynices the first born (*Oedipus at Colonus* 375, 1293-4).

27. Cf. Gantz 1993, vol. 2, 504.

28. See Griffith 1999 on Sophocles' *Antigone* 111.

29. Gantz 1993, vol. 2, 506.

30. Eteocles' decision has also been taken to refer to his lack of strategy in the sense of appointing defenders too late; for this view, see Aélion 1983, I, 203.

31. This scene has often been taken as spurious, that is, as a post-classical piece composed for independent production and later interpolated into the text of the *Phoenician Women*. The earliest criticism has been thought to be a scholium in the third hypothesis to the play, which remarks that 'Antigone looking from the wall is not part of the drama'. Much recent scholarship has argued against the authenticity of the scene, based on diction, dramatic logic and coherence, including Dihle 1981, 60-72. For a refutation of these reservations and the defence of the scene as Euripidean, see Erbse 1984, 237-47; Burgess 1987, who also argues (104) that the ancient critic's scholium is concerned not with textual criticism but with an evaluation of the play in terms of Aristotelian unity (cf. Mueller-Goldingen 1985, 52 n. 18, who interprets it as a literary-aesthetic remark); Mastronarde 1994, 168-73.

32. Aeschylus depicts the atmosphere of panic and confusion also by means of the metre, as the Chorus (78-108) use predominantly dochmiacs (instead of the usual spoken anapaests), a metre associated with agitation and wild emotion. Cf. Hutchinson 1985, 57.

33. Cf. Mastronarde 1994, 168.

34. Cf. Scodel 1997. On the pictorial aspect of this scene, see Barlow 1971, 57-60; Zeitlin 1994, 173-86.

35. The passage has been suspected as spurious. For arguments against deletion, see Craik 1988, 233-4, Mastronarde 1994, 456-9. On the shields and the semiotics of their emblems, see Zeitlin 1982, Goff 1988, Katsouris 1996, 45-8, Morin 2001.

36. See Mastronarde 1994, 459 and n. 1.

37. On this trick, see Borthwick 1970, 17-21.

38. See Mastronarde 1994, 528-9.

39. See Mastronarde 1994 on Euripides' *Phoenician Women* 1217-63n and on 1356-424; Amiech 2004, 529.

40. See Mastronarde 1994, 487.

41. For the presentation of the chieftains of the Argive expedition against Thebes in *Thebaid*, see Davies 1989, 25-8.

42. Mastronarde 1994, 168.

3. Characters and Actions

1. Cf. Méridier 1911, 65.
2. Cf. Falkner 1995, 196.
3. Falkner 1995, 196.
4. Foley 1985, 115.
5. Falkner 1995, 196.
6. For Jocasta's concern for Oedipus, cf. 53, 60, 1088-9 (which implies mutuality as when Oedipus is saddened after hearing of her death, 1566), 1693-5. See Craik 1988 on 1088-9; 1548-9.
7. Cf. Craik 1988 ad loc; Mastronarde 1994 ad loc.
8. Craik 1988, 172.
9. On Jocasta's role in the play in terms of her old age and motherhood, see Falkner 1995, 193-210. For a discussion of the Euripidean Jocasta, Aethra and Hecuba as three examples of maternal persuasion, see Foley 2001, 272-99.
10. Longo Rubbi 1967 (403-9) has alleged that there is a ritual apotropaic function in this dance, but the evidence is too scant to corroborate this. The author has also suggested (407) that, combined with magic incantation, Jocasta's dance is related to the spells asked for by the Messenger at 1260; but the Messenger's saying can refer to any means aiming at reconciliation and need not necessarily apply to magic. Cf. Mueller-Goldingen 1985, 76 n. 10; Mastronarde 1994 on 316; Amiech 2004, 308.
11. On the ritual acts in the play, see Sourvinou-Inwood 2003, 377-86.
12. For parallels, see Mastronarde 1994 on 1763.
13. Craik 1988 on 382.
14. Amiech 2004 on 382.
15. For Jocasta exile is similar to slavery (392), which recalls Antigone's fear of the fate of women after war (185-9). The theme of exile is used also at the end of the Menoeceus' episode (972-1018) and will play a major role in the *exodos* with regard to Oedipus and Antigone.
16. On this debate, see esp. Lloyd 1992, 83-93; de Romilly 1993.
17. Cf. Mastronarde 1994, 273.
18. Mastronarde 1986.
19. Mastronarde 1994 on 532.
20. Mastronarde 1994, 299-300. For aspects of the topicality of the play, see de Romilly 1965 (36-41 on *philotimia*); Delebecque 1951, 347-64; Goossens 1962, 600-22; Ebener 1964; Garlan 1966 (on military tactics).
21. Amiech 2004, 334.
22. Scharffenberger 1995.
23. On comic effects in Euripides see esp. Gregory 2000 and in Greek tragedy in general Seidensticker 1982.

24. As Craik 1988, 198, aptly notes, this idea may have been implied at the end of the prologue, where Jocasta prayed to Zeus for periodicity in human happiness (85-7).

25. For other philosophical parallels, see Mastronarde 1994 on 536. See also Mueller-Goldingen 1985, 104, for the influence of Pythagorean philosophy on Jocasta's view of equality.

26. For the idea of equality as informing the sophistic thought and the Athenian society, see Guthrie 1971, ch. 6.

27. Mastronarde 1994 on 539-40.

28. Both *nomimon* ('by law') and *monimon* ('lasting') are attested in manuscript tradition. Murray (1909), Mueller-Goldingen 1985 and Craik 1988 prefer reading *monimon*; Mastronarde 1994, Diggle 1994 and Amiech 2004 prefer *nomimon*, which makes better sense in the sophistic context of the preference of law over nature. See Mastronarde 1994 on 538.

29. For the advocates of nature in the controversy law *versus* nature, see Guthrie 1971, ch. 4.4.

30. For the relation between injustice and happiness, see Mastronarde 1994 on 549 and Amiech 2004 on 549.

31. Craik 1988 on 1259-60.

32. Falkner 1995, 205.

33. Falkner 1995, 206.

34. On female death in Greek tragedy, as well as on 'masculine' *versus* 'feminine' ways of death, see in general Loraux (1987). On suicide in Greek tragedy, see in general Garrison 1995.

35. Mastronarde 1994 on 1574.

36. The participle *marnamenous*, 'fighting' at 1574, if referring to *tekna*, 'children', 1570, and having taken the masculine form under the influence of the masculine *leontas*, 'lions', may refer to an act completed. The timeless present here was suggested by Wilamowitz, for which see Mastronarde on 1574.

37. For references, see Mueller-Goldingen 1985, 70 n. 1; Amiech 2004, 299. For a comparison of Polynices with the Spartan ambassador in Aristophanes' *Lysistrata*, see Scharffenberger 1995. Luschnig 1995, 199, associates instead his stealthy entrance with the *ephebeia* process, that is, the young men coming of age, though one may counterargue that Polynices is an adult.

38. Craik 1988, 244.

39. Mastronarde 1994, 528-9.

40. Mueller-Goldingen 1985, 78 n. 14.

41. This is well reflected in Euripides' *Ion* (673-5), where Ion remarks that a foreigner in Athens has no freedom of speech.

42. Mastronarde 1994 on 395.

43. See Mastronarde 1994, on 438-42; Amiech 2004, on 438-42.

44. Mastronarde 1986, 205 and 210 n. 18; Mastronarde 1994, 271.
45. On Polynices' hypocrisy and selfishness, see Saïd 1985, 512-13.
46. Cf. Mastronarde 1994, 271.
47. Contrary to critics who saw in Polynices a thoroughly sympathetic character, de Romilly 1965, 31, rightly remarked that it is often forgotten that both Eteocles and Polynices are guilty.
48. On Polynices' and Eteocles' both being unjust, cf. Dubischar 2001, 363. See also Kosak 2004, 181, for both brothers sharing the same identity in excess.
49. See Mastronarde 1994 on 539-40 and on 509-10. Cf. Lloyd 1992, 89.
50. The cautious Creon and the rash Eteocles have sometimes reminded critics of the debate between the cautious Nicias and the rash Alcibiades of the Sicilian expedition (Thucydides 6.9ff.). See Craik 1988 on 692-3. On the topicality of the military debate, see Garlan 1966. But apart from similarities with military tactics known to the Athenian audience (cf. Mastronarde 1994 on 724-31) the general juxtaposition between hastiness and prudence is a *topos*; cf. Mastronarde 1994 on 746; Amiech 2004, 402.
51. On this play, see Collard, Cropp and Lee 1995, 148-94.
52. The authenticity of this scene, either in part or in totality, has often been questioned, principally because of its strong resemblance to Sophocles' *Antigone*. For a review of the debate, see Craik 1988, 245; Mastronarde 1994, 591-4; Amiech 2004, 567. On the proliferation of characters and themes in the *exodos*, see Dunn 1996, 180-202.
53. See the diagram of Theban genealogy in the Appendix.
54. Craik 1988 on 984.
55. See Wilkins 1990, 180-1.
56. These lines have often been suspected as histrionic interpolation. See e.g. Mueller-Goldingen 1985, 159; Mastronarde 2004 on 1013-18. For a defence of these lines, which were not suspected in antiquity, see Craik 1988 on 1012; Amiech 2004 on 1013-18.
57. Translation by Collard, Cropp and Lee 1995, in Aris & Phillips.
58. On human sacrifice in Euripides, see esp. O'Connor-Visser 1987 and Wilkins 1990. On Menoeceus' self-sacrifice as a noble suicide, see Garrison 1995, 138-44.
59. See Mastronarde 1994, 392.
60. Falkner 1995, 199.
61. Falkner 1995, 208-9.
62. This scene resembles Antigone's resolve at the end of Aeschylus' *Seven against Thebes* (1035-6), where the decree is issued not by Creon but by the Council of the city (1012). This is part of the final scene of the Aeschylean play, which many critics have regarded as an interpo-

lation modelled on the scene from the *Phoenician Women*. See Hutchinson 1985 on Aeschylus' *Seven against Thebes* 1005-78.

63. A scholium on 1692 does not understand that Antigone abandons the idea of the burial for the idea of exile and thus wrongly accuses Euripides for inconsistency, followed and modified by modern critics who believe that the mixture of themes is the result of interpolation (for a defence of the consistency, see Conacher 1967b, 97-101 and Mastronarde 1994, 592 and notes). The authenticity of lines 1743-6, where Antigone says that she will bury Polynices, is suspect (see Conacher 1967b, 100-1 and n. 13; Mastronarde 1994 on 1744).

64. Cf. Aélion 1983, vol. 1, 222.

65. For Messenger narratives in Greek tragedy, see esp. de Jong 1991 and Barrett 2002.

66. For the limited presence of first-person in both Messengers' narratives, cf. Barrett 2002, 83-6.

67. Mastronarde 1994 on 1335.

68. de Jong 1991, 141-2.

69. On this symmetry, see Girard 1977, 44-5.

70. Craik 1988, 244 and on 1421.

71. Cf. de Jong 1991: 27.

4. The Choral Odes

1. On the tragic Chorus in general the seminal study is Kranz 1933. See also Hose 1990 and 1991; Bacon 1995; Calame 1995; Gould 1996; Goldhill 1996; Mastronarde 1998. On ancient views of the tragic Chorus often reflected in the scholia, see Gentili 1984-5. On the Chorus in the *Phoenician Women*, see Parry 1963, 53-242; Conacher 1967, 245-8; Arthur 1977; Mastronarde 1984-5; Luschnig 1995, 195-8, 213-15, 219-21, 225-6, 230-1 and the relevant sections in the commentaries by Mueller-Goldingen 1985, Craik 1988, Mastronarde 1994.

2. See Kranz 1933, 111, for the similarities in rhythm between the *parodoi* of the two plays.

3. See Arthur 1977, 168. Arthur's reading of the choral odes throughout the article is based on the idea that the curse that was originally attached to Cadmus extends down to Menoeceus and Oedipus' sons.

4. The technique of linking choral odes through the narration of correlated events is used also in Euripides' *Trojan Women* and employed by Aeschylus in his *Agamemnon* and *Seven against Thebes*. Cf. Battezzato 2005, 159.

5. On the ambivalent aspect of the *Spartoi*, see Natanblut 2005, 46-7 and 65-6.

6. Cf. Hose 1990, 147 n. 32. On Ares in the *Phoenician Women*, see Masaracchia 1987.

7. Cf. Arthur 1977, 168 n. 19.

8. Cf. Masarrachia 1987, 175.

9. On the mutual killings of the *Spartoi* as an example from the past applicable to Eteocles and Polynices, see Parry 1963, 188.

10. For the invocation of Epaphus in Aeschylus' *Suppliants* 40-57 as a precedent, see Willink 2002, 714.

11. For the specific echoing of the preceding debate between the brothers, see Hose 1991, 163.

12. This is an example of the play's emphasis on the idea of joyless music and dance, which starts with Jocasta's monody (301-54) and is mirrored in Antigone's monody (1485-1538) and her expressed abandonment in the *exodos* (cf. 1754-7) of her youthful songs and dances now that she calls herself in a dance for corpses 'bacchant of dead'. On joyless dance as a motif in the play, see Podlecki 1962, 369-72.

13. Cf. Arthur 1977, 177.

14. On *eris* and Ares, see Masarrachia 1987, 176-7. On the resemblance of the attack of the Sphinx on the Theban walls with that of the attack of an invading army, see Parry 1963, 194.

15. Especially in his late plays and under the influence of the musician Timotheus, Euripides composed *stasima* which sometimes seem to be independent. An early example of the condemnation of Euripides' *stasima* as dramatically irrelevant, which refers in particular to the *Phoenician Women*, is the scholium on Aristophanes' *Acharnians* 443, which uses the *stasima* of this tragedy as an example of Euripides' tendency to compose choral odes which have no dramatic relevance but consist in mere narration of stories. Dramatic relevance is present, however, but often it has to be reconstructed as Euripides frequently relies on allusion.

16. Oedipus' sons too try to be victorious (cf. 781, 1252-3, 1374-6) but fail. For the use of *kallinikos* in the play, see Podlecki 1962, 367-9; Luschnig 1995, 223 and n. 155, where she also notes the ironical use of the same epithet in Euripidean plays like *Medea*, *Heracles* and *Electra*.

17. Cf. Mastronarde 1994 on 1066.

18. See Masarrachia 1987, 179 and 180, for the idea that Ares may be implied both behind the coming of Sphinx as well as behind the 'gods' who prohibited Laius from procreation.

19. Cf. 379, where Jocasta remarks that 'some god' destroys Oedipus' family.

20. The Chorus now come to voice something that was only alluded in the dialogue between Jocasta and Polynices. There Polynices said that the fight between himself and Tydeus (an early mirroring of the fight between Eteocles and Polynices) made Adrastus liken them to beasts (421). This causes surprise to Jocasta but it is an early hint at the ferocity of Polynices, which will be shared by his brother, and will attribute them the kind of savagery that is associated with Theban past. For Foley (1985, 143 n. 143) the Chorus' reference here 'underlines their final absorption into Theban myth'.

21. On the beast-imagery of the play, see Podlecki 1962, 362-7. On the beast-imagery as a recurrent Euripidean motif in his later plays, notably *Ion, Orestes* and *Bacchae*, see Burian and Swann 1981, 12-13.

22. Cf. Rehm 2003, 43.

23. Cf. Falkner 1995, 209-10.

5. Performance

1. This field of research in Greek tragedy was pioneered by Taplin 1977 and 1978, followed (and occasionally challenged) by several scholars, esp. Wiles 1997 and Rehm 2002. For accounts of Euripidean stagecraft in general, see Hourmouziades 1965; Halleran 1985. For brief accounts of the characteristics of the original performance of the *Phoenician Women*, see Craik 1988, 45-6; Mastronarde 1994, 14-16; Amiech 2004, 47-53. For the use of space and of significant actions in the play, see Jouanna 1976 and Altena 2000 respectively.

2. On silent extras in Euripides, see Stanley-Porter 1973.

3. Craik 1988, 46; cf. Mastronarde 1994, 16 and n. 1 for alternatives.

4. Amiech 2004, 48 and n. 123.

5. On the music of tragedy, see Csapo-Slater 1995, 331-43; Wilson 2005. The standard musical instrument used in tragedy was the *aulos* (flute or pipe), which had musical flexibility and ability to imitate many sounds.

6. On physical contact in Greek tragedy, see Kaimio 1988.

7. By Hellenistic times it had become a convention that the *parodos* on the spectators' right led to the city whereas the one on the left led to the countryside or harbour. For the fifth century one has to assume that the director was consistent in his association of each side-entrance with a specific location (Sommerstein 2002, 9)

8. Brooke 1962, 104, suggests that the Chorus' oriental costume may have been of the Asiatic type, familiar from representations of Medea, or of the Egyptian type worn by the Danaids.

9. See Mastronarde 1990. On the use of the palace roof in the *Phoenician Women* by Pollux to refer to a two-storey scene-building (a post-classical use), see Poe 2000.

10. Cf. Walcot 1976, 69; Amiech 2004 on 301-3.

11. Mastronarde 1994 on 316.

12. Altena 2000, 318.

13. Cf. Altena 2000, 314.

14. Cf. Altena 2000, 313.

15. See Amiech 2004, 371. This type of spoken parts accompanied by music is often called *parakatalogê*; see Battezzato 2005, 151.
16. Willink 1990, 201 n. 53.
17. The scholium on 690 and Craik 1988 on 690ff.
18. Mastronarde 1994 and Amiech 2004 on 690.
19. Craik 1988 on 778 sqq; Mastronarde 1994 on 779.
20. Mastronarde 1994 on 838.
21. Mastronarde 1994, 396.
22. Jouanna 1976, 88-90.
23. Mastronarde 1994, 396.
24. Kaimio 1988, 57.
25. Mastronarde 1994 on 953.
26. Amiech 2004, 50-1, 468.
27. Mastronarde 1994 on 1213.
28. See Mastronarde 1994 on 1308, where he also argues against the view that Menoeceus' body is carried onstage.
29. Cf. Flickinger 1918, 222.
30. Mastronarde 1994 on 1539.
31. Jouanna 1976, 94.
32. Mastronarde 1994 on 1720-1.
33. See Mastronarde 1994 ad loc.
34. Jouanna 1976, 84-5 and n. 12.

6. Reception

1. Overall, the popularity of Euripides' *Phoenician Women* across different periods and different countries testifies to its vigour and influence. Its depth of content, its diction as well as its dramatization of fundamental issues concerning human behaviour within a familial and a civic context had something to say to each subsequent era according to the aesthetics and the socio-political circumstances each time.
2. On the adaptation of Theban myths in the Middle Ages, see Battles 2004. On the myth in the Arts from 1300 to the 1900s, see Davidson Reid 1993, vol. 2, 989-92.
3. See Bremer 1983b, 281, 284 and n. 4. Cf. Cribiore 2001, 243-4.
4. On the popularity of Euripidean plays from the fourth century BC onwards, see Kuch 1978.
5. On the popularity of the play in late antiquity, see esp. Bremer 1983b. On the rich textual tradition of the play, see Mastronarde and Bremer 1982 (402-29 list the testimonia); Bremer 1983 and Bremer and Worps 1986. See also Amiech 2004, 53-6 and Craik 1988, 51 and passim in the commentary.
6. See Amiech 2004, 55 and on 1354-5.
7. See Craik 1988 on 1595-614 and on 460-1.

8. See Cartledge 1997, 11.
9. See Mastronarde 1988, 14.
10. See Bremer 1983b and esp. Cribiore 2001, who discusses several papyri containing school exercises on the *Phoenician Women*.
11. See Amiech 2004, 54-5.
12. See Amiech 2004, 54 and 21 n. 31.
13. See Bremer 1983b, 287 and Mastronarde 1994 on 395.
14. See Braund 1997, who draws parallels between Pyrrhus on the one hand and Eteocles and Oedipus on the other.
15. See Bremer 1983b, 287-8.
16. On the echoes of the Menoeceus episode after Euripides, see Amiech 2004, 57-8.
17. *LIMC*, vol. 4.1, s.v. 'Eteokles', no 2. See Small 1981, 14-15, no. 7, pl. 4b. For other representations of Eteocles and Polynices stabbing each other as in Euripides' play, see *LIMC* vol. 4.1, s.v. 'Eteocles', nos 18-24.
18. Webster ²1967, 163.
19. *LIMC*, vol. 4.1, s.v. 'Eteokles', no 10. See Small 1981, pl. 44b.
20. British Museum, London F 338. See Webster ²1967, 162.
21. British Museum, London, G 104, *LIMC*, vol. 1.1., s.v. 'Antigone', nos 6 and 9.
22. See Jouanna 1976, 86-7 and Fig. 1; Jouanna suggests (87) that the artist may have depicted both scenes of supplication in order to convey the contrast and the pathos involved. See also Walters 1894, 326; Mastronarde 1994, 414.
23. See Walters 1894, 326.
24. *LIMC* 4.1, s.v. 'Eteocles', nos 13 and 14.
25. Webster ²1967, 163.
26. London, G 105. See Murray 1888, Webster ²1967, 163 and Mastronarde 1994, 625.
27. *LIMC* 7.1, s.v. 'Oidipous', nos 96-7.
28. Dangel 1995.
29. See the discussion in Mueller-Goldingen 1985, 39.
30. See Frank 1995, 44. On Accius' version, see Frank 1995, 25-7.
31. For a comparative analysis, see Mueller-Goldingen 1995 and Frank 1995, 21-5. On the complex issue of Seneca's relation to literary tradition, see Tarrant 1978.
32. On this device see Frank 1995, 4 and 78 and Frank 1995b.
33. These verses recall the Euripidean Eteocles' 'let the whole house be damned' and Creon's 'let the city go' in Euripides' *Phoenician Women* 624 and 919 respectively. Translations from the Senecan play will be quoted from Fitch 2002.
34. On reading echoes of Stoicism as well as for the limits of this approach, see Frank 1995, 31 and notes on Seneca's *Phoenissae* 77-9, 188-201.

35. See Craik 1988 on 1526-7.
36. See esp. Vessey 1973, 67-71 and for Statius' use of other material in general see Smolenaars 1994, xxvi-xlii. For specific associations between passages in Statius and Euripides' *Phoenician Women*, see more recently Fernandelli 2000, on the influence of the Euripidean description of Adrastus' and Hippomedon's shields on the description of Capaneus' shield in Statius, *Thebaid* 4.165-72.
37. For these translations, see Burian 1997, 232.
38. See Burian 1997, 232-3, referring also to Mueller 1980, who focuses on the function of Greek tragedy in the period 1550-1800.
39. See Gascoigne 1907-10, vol. 1.
40. See Beyerle 1973, 21 n. 30 and O'Donnell 1954.
41. Racine also employs elements from the *Phoenician Women* in his *Marie Stuart*; see Beyerle 1973, 21 and n. 30.
42. Cf. Beyerle 1973, 9 n. 1.
43. For a comparative analysis of Euripides' and Racine's plays see Osho 1977/78. See also Beyerle 1973, 109-48 and Goodkin 1991, 47-79.
44. Cf. Mastronarde 1994 on 438-42.
45. See Hall 1999b, 65 and Hall and Macintosh 2005, 43-4.
46. Hall and Macintosh 2005, 191 and 566.
47. See Hall and Macintosh 2005, 272-4.
48. On this play, see Hall and Macintosh 2005, 293-300.
49. For an overview of performances of Euripides' *Phoenician Women* in Greece until 1988, with information drawn from the programmes preserved at the 'Archive of Programmes of the Museum and Centre for the Study of Greek Theatre' at Athens, see Mavromoustakos et al. 1993.
50. The music can be found in the double CD of Fm-records (1999), Athens, including the libretto and photos.
51. See Mikis Theodorakis' discussion of *Antigone* at www.mikis-theodorakis.net/mikant-e.html
52. It was recorded in concert at the Pallas Theatre, Athens, in May 1987 and released in CD by MBI records company in the same year.
53. For this German production, see Flashar 1991, 268-9.
54. Macintosh 1997, 321 and n. 58. See also the reviews by Edith Hall in the *Times Literary Supplement* 4832 (November 1995) 35 and by Kalina Stafanova in *European Cultural Review* 15 (2004).
55. See the articles by Lesley McDowell in *The Independent* of 5 July 2003; Lynne Walker in *The Independent* of 13 August 2003; Rhiannon Batten in *The Independent* of 22 August 2003; Lyn Gardner in the *Guardian* of 7 August 2003.
56. See the review by Macey Levin in the Internet Theatre Magazine *Curtain Up* (www.curtainup.com/phoenician women.html).

Guide to Further Reading

Editions and commentaries

L.C. Valckenaer (1755), *Euripidis Tragoedia, Phoenissae*. Leyde. A commentary in Latin with a translation in Latin by H. Grotius.

G. Murray (1909), *Euripidis Fabulae*, III. Oxford: Oxford UP (Oxford Classical Texts). A critical edition of the Euripidean text in the Oxford Classical Text series.

A.C. Pearson (1909), *Euripides, The Phoenissae*. Cambridge: Cambridge UP. An early English commentary on the play, with a focus on textual issues.

J.U. Powell (1911), *The Phoenissae of Euripides*. London: Constable & Company Ltd. [repr. 1979 by Arno Press]. An early English commentary on the play, focusing particularly on the issue of interpolation.

L. Méridier and F. Chapouthier (1950), *Les Phéniciennes*, in *Euripide*, V. Paris: Les Belles Letters. A critical edition of the Greek text with translation in French

C. Mueller-Goldingen (1985), *Untersuchungen zu den Phönissen des Euripides*. Stuttgart: Franz Steiner. A literary commentary on the play discussing each scene successively and focusing on textual and dramatic issues.

D.J. Mastronarde (1988), *Phoenissae*. Leipzig: Teubner. Donald Mastronarde has worked extensively on the textual tradition of Euripides' *Phoenician Women* (cf. D.J. Mastronarde and J.M. Bremer, *The Textual Tradition of Euripides' Phoinissai*. Berkeley: University of California Publications: Classical Studies, 27) and this book is his edition of the text for the Teubner series. There are some differences from the then forthcoming text by James Diggle (1994, see below) and Mastronarde adhered to his own critical edition in his 1994 commentary (see below). In accordance with the Teubner series the book provides a long bibliography on the play.

E. Craik (1988), *Euripides: Phoenician Women*. Warminster: Aris & Phillips. Following a brief introduction to the play, the Greek text is faced on the opposite page by an excellent English prose translation, followed by a rich commentary.

J. Diggle (1994), *Euripidis Fabulae*, III. Oxford: Oxford UP (Oxford Classical Texts). The standard Euripidean text in the Oxford Classical Texts series.

D.J. Mastronarde (1994), *Euripides: Phoenissae*. Cambridge: Cambridge UP. A critical edition of the Greek text, with a brief introduction and a learned philological and literary commentary on the play.

D. Kovacs (2002), *Euripides: Helen, Phoenician Women, Orestes*. Cambridge, MA: Harvard UP (The Loeb Classical Library). An edition of the Greek text, with a facing English translation which follows closely the original without losing a lively tone.

C. Amiech (2004), *Les Phéniciennes d' Euripide*. Paris: L' Harmattan. A detailed and informative book on the literary aspects of the play as well as on the history of its text, consisting in an introduction, Greek text faced by a translation in French and commentary.

E. Medda (2006), *Euripide: Le Fenicie*. Biblioteca Universale Rizzoli. Milano: RCS Libri. The most recent book on the Euripidean play, with introduction, Greek text and facing Italian translation and a commentary. (This book appeared after the present volume was completed and so no references are made to it in the main text.)

English translations

E. Wychoff (1959), *The Phoenician Women*, in D. Grene and R. Lattimore (eds), *The Complete Greek Tragedies, Euripides V: Electra, The Phoenician Women, the Bacchae*. Chicago and London: The University of Chicago Press. An old translation with simple language in verse.

P. Burian and B. Swann (1981), *Euripides: The Phoenician Women*. Oxford and New York: Oxford UP. A vivid translation, which tries to evoke the dramatic atmosphere of the original. It also includes a short, critical introduction to the play and stage directions, as well as a glossary of mythical references.

E. Craik (1988) see above under 'Editions and commentaries'.

R. Elman (1998), *The Phoenician Women*, in D.R. Slavitt and P. Bovie (eds), *Euripides, 3: Alcestis, Daughters of Troy, The Phoenician Women, Iphigenia at Aulis, Rhesus*. Philadelphia: University of Pennsylvania Press. A faithful translation by a poet and novelist of the original text in vivid verse aiming at being suitable for the stage.

D. Kovacs (2002) see above under 'Editions and commentaries'.

The reception of Euripides' *Phoenician Women*

D. von Beyerle (1973), *Die feindlichen Brüder von Aeschylus bis Alfieri*. Berlin: Walter De Gruyter. A study of the myth of Oedipus' sons in

Aeschylus, Euripides, Seneca, Statius, Garnier, Rotrou, Racine and Alfieri, with a useful bibliography.

D. Braund (1997), 'Plutarch's *Pyrrhus* and Euripides' *Phoenician Women*: Biography and Tragedy on Pleonectic Parenting', *Histos* 1, 1-11. An examination of the influence of the Euripidean play on the central theme of pleonectic ambition in Plutarch's *Pyrrhus*.

J.M. Bremer (1983), 'The Popularity of Euripides' *Phoenissae* in Late Antiquity', in *Actes du VIIe Congrès de la Federation Internationale des Associations d' Études Classiques*, vol. 1, 281-8. Budapest. A survey of the popularity of the Euripidean play in late antiquity, esp. in Roman times, with a discussion of the evidence provided by manuscripts and papyri.

R. Cribiore (2001), 'The Grammarian's Choice: The Popularity of Euripides' *Phoenissae* in Hellenistic and Roman Education', in Y.L. Too (ed.), *Education in Greek and Roman Antiquity*, 241-60. Leiden: Brill. A discussion of the use of the Euripidean play for educational purposes, focusing on several school exercises preserved in papyri.

P. Mavromoustakos et al. (1993), 'Performance History' in K. Τοπούζης (K. Topouzis), transl. *ΕΥΡΙΠΙΔΗΣ, ΦΟΙΝΙΣΣΑΙ*. Athens: Epikairotêta (Ancient Greek Theatre, 28), 199-224. A brief history of performances of Euripides' *Phoenician Women* in Greek, with information on cast and director, accompanied by photos.

C. Mueller-Goldingen (1995), 'Seneca und Euripides. Zur Rezeptionsgeschichte der *Phönissen*', *Rheinisches Museum für Philologie* 138, 82-92. A comparative analysis between the Euripidean and the Senecan tragedies.

Open University, London, England: Research Project on the Reception of the Texts and Images of Ancient Greece in modern literature (www2.open.ac.uk/ClassicalStudies/GreekPlays). A data-base of productions of ancient plays with extensive reviews where available.

J.M. Osho (1977/78), 'Euripides' *Phoenissae* and Racine's *La Thèbaide*: A Comparative Analysis', *Museum Africum* 6, 82-93. A comparative analysis between the Euripidean play and Racine's tragedy.

Oxford Archive of Performances of Greek and Roman Drama (APGRD) (www.apgrd.ox.ac.uk). A database of productions of Greek and Roman drama in all languages from 1460 to the present.

Bibliography

R. Aélion (1983), *Euripide: Héritier d' Eschyle*. 2 vols. Paris: Les Belles Lettres.

W. Allan (2000), 'Euripides and the Sophists: Society and the Theatre of War', in M.J. Cropp et al. (eds), 145-56. Champaign, IL (*Illinois Classical Studies*, 1999-2000).

G. Allen (2000), *Intertextuality*. London: Routledge.

H. Altena (2000), 'Text and Performance: On Significant Actions in Euripides' *Phoenissae*', in M.J. Cropp et al. (eds), 303-23. Champaign, IL (*Illinois Classical Studies*, 1999-2000).

C. Amiech (2004) (ed.), *Les Phéniciennes d' Euripide*. Paris: L' Harmattan.

M.J. Anderson (2005), 'Myth', in J. Gregory (ed.), 121-35. Malden, MA and Oxford: Blackwell.

M.B. Arthur (1977), 'The Curse of Civilization. The Choral Odes of the *Phoenissae*', *Harvard Studies in Classical Philology* 81, 163-85.

H. Bacon (1995), 'The Chorus in Greek Life and Drama', *Arion* 3, 6-24.

H.C. Baldry (1956), 'The Dramatization of the Theban Legend', *Greece and Rome* 3, 24-37.

S.A. Barlow (1971), *The Imagery of Euripides: A Study in the Dramatic Use of Pictorial Language*. London: Methuen.

J. Barrett (2002), *Staged Narrative: Poetics and the Messenger in Greek Tragedy*. Berkeley: University of California Press.

L. Battezzato (2005), 'Lyric', in J. Gregory (ed.), 149-66. Malden, MA and Oxford: Blackwell.

D. Battles (2004), *The Medieval Tradition of Thebes: History and Narrative in the Roman de Thèbes, Boccaccio, Chaucer, and Lydgate*. New York: Routledge.

V. Bers (1994), 'Tragedy and Rhetoric', in I. Worthington (ed.), *Greek Rhetoric in Action*, 176-95. London: Routledge.

D. von Beyerle (1973), *Die feindlichen Brüder von Aeschylus bis Alfieri*. Berlin: Walter De Gruyter.

E.K. Borthwick (1970), 'Two Scenes of Combat in Euripides', *Journal of Hellenic Studies* 90, 15-21.

D. Braund (1997), 'Plutarch's *Pyrrhus* and Euripides' *Phoenician Women*: Biography and Tragedy on Pleonectic Parenting', *Histos* 1, 1-11.

Bibliography

J.M. Bremer (1983), 'Papyri Containing Fragments of Eur. *Phoenissae*', *Mnemosyne* 36: 293-305.

J.M. Bremer (1983b), 'The Popularity of Euripides' *Phoenissae* in Late Antiquity', in *Actes du VIIe Congrès de la Federation Internationale des Associations d' Études Classiques*, vol. 1, 281-8. Budapest.

J.M. Bremer and K.A. Worps (1986), 'Papyri Containing Fragments of Eur. *Phoenissae* (2)', *Mnemosyne* 39: 278-87.

D.L. Burgess (1987), 'The Authenticity of the Teichoskopia of Euripides' *Phoenissae*', *Classical Journal* 83, 103-13.

P. Burian (1997), 'Tragedy Adapted for Stages and Screens: The Renaissance to the Present', in P.E. Easterling (ed.), 228-83. Cambridge: Cambridge UP.

P. Burian and B. Swann (1981), 'Introduction', in *Euripides: The Phoenician Women*, 3-17. Oxford and New York: Oxford UP.

R. Bushnell (1988), *Prophesying Tragedy: Sign and Voice in Sophocles' Theban Plays*. Ithaca & London: Cornell UP.

R. Buxton (1982), *Persuasion in Greek Tragedy*. Cambridge: Cambridge UP.

C. Calame (1995), 'From Choral Poetry to Tragic Stasimon: the Enactment of Women's Songs', *Arion* 3, 136-54.

P. Cartledge, '"Deep Plays": Theatre as Process in Greek Civic Life', in P.E. Easterling (ed.), 3-35. Cambridge: Cambridge UP:

C. Collard (1975), 'Formal Debates in Euripides' Drama', *Greece and Rome* 22, 58-71. [repr. (with an *addendum*), in J. Mossman (ed.), 64-80. Oxford: Oxford UP.]

C. Collard (1981), *Euripides*. Oxford: Oxford UP.

C. Collard, M.J. Cropp and J. Gibert (2004) (eds), *Euripides: Selected Fragmentary Plays*, II. Warminster: Aris & Phillips.

C. Collard, M.J. Cropp and K.H. Lee (1995) (eds), *Euripides: Selected Fragmentary Plays*, I. Warminster: Aris & Phillips.

D.J. Conacher (1967), *Euripidean Drama: Myth, Theme, and Structure*. Toronto: University of Toronto Press.

D.J. Conacher (1967b), 'Themes in the *Exodus* of Euripides' *Phoenissae*', *Phoenix* 21, 92-101.

D.J. Conacher (1981), 'Rhetoric and Relevance in Euripidean Drama', *American Journal of Philology* 102, 3-25. [repr. in J. Mossman (ed.), 81-101. Oxford: Oxford UP.]

D.J. Conacher (1998), *Euripides and the Sophists: Some Dramatic Treatments of Philosophical Ideas*. London: Duckworth.

E. Craik (1988) (ed.), *Euripides: Phoenician Women*. Warminster: Aris & Phillips.

R. Cribiore (2001), 'The Grammarian's Choice: the Popularity of Euripides' *Phoenissae* in Hellenistic and Roman Education', in Y.L.

Bibliography

Too (ed.), *Education in Greek and Roman Antiquity*, 241-60. Leiden: Brill.

N.T. Croally (1994), *Euripidean Polemic: The Trojan Women and the Function of Tragedy*. Cambridge: Cambridge UP.

M.J. Cropp (2005), 'Lost Tragedies: A Survey', in J. Gregory (ed.), 271-92. Malden, MA and Oxford: Blackwell.

M.J. Cropp et al. (2000) (eds), *Euripides and Tragic Theatre in the Late Fifth Century*. Champaign, IL (*Illinois Classical Studies*, 1999-2000).

E. Csapo and W.J. Slater (1995), *The Context of Ancient Drama*. Ann Arbor: University of Michigan Press.

J. Dangel (1995) (ed.), *Accius, Fragments*. Paris: Les Belles Lettres.

J. Davidson Reid (1993), *The Oxford Guide to Classical Mythology in the Arts, 1300-1990s*. 2 vols. New York and Oxford: Oxford UP.

M. Davies (1989), *The Greek Epic Cycle*. London: Bristol Classical Press.

E. Delebecque (1951), *Euripide et la Guerre du Péloponnèse*. Paris: Librairie C. Klincksieck.

J. Diggle (1994) (ed.), *Euripidis Fabulae,* vol. III. Oxford: Oxford UP (Oxford Classical Texts).

J. Diggle (1999), 'Euripides the Psychologist', in S. Patsalidis and E. Sakellaridou (eds), *(Dis)Placing Classical Greek Theatre*, 287-96. Thessaloniki: University Studio Press.

A. Dihle (1981), 'Der Prolog der *Bakchen* und die antike Überlieferung des Euripides-Textes', *Sitzungsberichte der Heidelberger Akademie der Wissenschaften, Philosophisch-historische Klasse* 2, 51-116.

M. Dubishar (2001), *Die Agonszenen bei Euripides: Untersuchungen zu ausgewählten* Dramen. Stuttgart: Metzler.

J. Duchemin (1945), *L' Agôn dans la Tragédie Grecque*. Paris: Les Belles Lettres.

F.M. Dunn (1996), *Tragedy's End: Closure and Innovation in Euripidean Drama*. New York and Oxford: Oxford UP.

P.E. Easterling (1997) (ed.), *The Cambridge Companion to Greek Tragedy*. Cambridge: Cambridge UP.

P.E. Easterling (1997b), 'From Repertoire to Canon', in P.E. Easterling (ed.), 211-27. Cambridge: Cambridge UP.

D. Ebener (1964), 'Die *Phönizierinnen* des Euripides als Spiegelbild geschichtlicher Wirklichkeit', *Eirene* 2, 72-9.

R. Eisner (1979), 'Euripides' Use of Myth', *Arethusa* 12, 153-74.

H. Erbse (1966), 'Beiträge zum Verständnis der euripideischen *Phoinissen*', *Philologus* 110, 1-34.

H. Erbse (1984), *Studien zum Prolog der euripideischen Tragödie. Untersuchungen zur antiken Literatur und Geschichte*, Band 20. Berlin: Walter de Gruyter.

Bibliography

T.M. Falkner (1995), 'Euripides and the Tragedy of Old Age: *Children of Heracles* and *Phoenician Women*', in T.M. Falkner (ed.), *The Poetics of Old Age in Greek Epic, Lyric, and Tragedy*, 169-210. Norman & London: University of Oklahoma Press.

M. Fernadelli (2000), 'Statius' *Thebaid* and Euripides' *Phoenissae* 1113-18', *Symbolae Osloenses* 75, 89-98.

J.G. Fitch (2002) (ed. and transl.) *Seneca: Hercules, Trojan Women, Phoenician Women, Medea, Phaedra*. Cambridge, MA: Harvard UP.

H. Flashar (1991), *Inszenierung der Antike: Das griechische Drama auf der Bühne der Neuzeit 1585-1990*. Munich: C.H. Beck.

R.C. Flickinger (1918), *The Greek Theater and its Drama*. Chicago and London: The University of Chicago Press.

H.P. Foley (1985), *Ritual Irony: Poetry and Sacrifice in Euripides*. Ithaca: Cornell UP.

H.P. Foley (2001), *Female Acts in Greek Tragedy*. Princeton: Princeton UP.

M. Frank (1995), *Seneca's Phoenissae. Introduction and Commentary*. Leiden: Brill.

M. Frank (1995b), 'The Rhetorical Use of Family Terms in Seneca's *Oedipus* and *Phoenissae*', *Phoenix* 49, 121-30.

T. Gantz (1993), *Early Greek Myth: A Guide to Literary and Artistic Sources*, vol. 2. Baltimore and London: The Johns Hopkins UP.

Y. Garlan (1966), 'De la Poliorcétique dans les *Phéniciennes* d' Euripide', *Revue des Études Anciennes* 68, 264-77.

E.P. Garrison (1995), *Groaning Tears: Ethical and Dramatic Aspects of Suicide in Greek Tragedy*. Leiden: Brill.

G. Gascoigne (1907-1910), *The Posies*, in J.W. Cunliffe (ed.), *The Complete Works of George Gascoigne*. 2 vols. Cambridge: Cambridge UP.

B. Gentili (1984-5), 'Il Coro Tragico nella Teoria degli Antichi', *Dioniso* 55, 17-35.

R. Girard (1977), *Violence and the Sacred*, transl. P. Gregory. Baltimore: The Johns Hopkins UP.

B.E. Goff (1988), 'The Shields of *Phoenissae*', *Greek, Roman and Byzantine Studies* 29, 135-52.

S. Goldhill (1986), *Reading Greek Tragedy*. Cambridge: Cambridge UP.

S. Goldhill (1996), 'Collectivity and Otherness: The Authority of the Tragic Chorus.' Response to Gould, in M.S. Silk (ed.), 244-56. Oxford: Clarendon Press.

S. Goldhill and R. Osborne (1999) (eds), *Performance Culture and Athenian Democracy*. Cambridge: Cambridge UP.

R.E. Goodkin (1991), *The Tragic Middle: Racine, Aristotle, Euripides*. Madison: The University of Wisconsin Press.

R. Goossens (1962), *Euripide et Athènes*. Brussels: Academie Royale de Belgique.

A. Gostoli (1978), 'Some Aspects of the Theban Myth in the Lille Stesichorus', *Greek, Roman and Byzantine Studies* 19, 23-7.

J. Gould (1996), 'Tragedy and Collective Experience', in M.S. Silk (ed.), 217-43. Oxford: Clarendon Press.

J. Gregory (1991), *Euripides and the Instruction of the Athenians*. Ann Arbor: University of Michigan Press.

J. Gregory (2000), 'Comic Elements in Euripides', in M.J. Cropp et al. (eds), 59-74. Champaign, IL (*Illinois Classical Studies*, 1999-2000).

J. Gregory (2005) (ed.), *A Companion to Greek Tragedy*. Malden, MA and Oxford: Blackwell.

J. Gregory (2005b), 'Euripidean Tragedy', in J. Gregory (ed.), 251-70. Malden, MA and Oxford: Blackwell.

M. Griffith (1999) (ed.), *Sophocles: Antigone*. Cambridge: Cambridge UP.

W.K.C. Guthrie (1971), *The Sophists*. Cambridge: Cambridge UP.

E. Hall (1989), *Inventing the Barbarian. Greek Self-definition Through Tragedy*. Oxford: Oxford UP.

E. Hall (1997), 'The Sociology of Athenian Tragedy', in P.E. Easterling (ed.), 93-126. Cambridge: Cambridge UP.

E. Hall (1999b), 'Greek Tragedy and the British Stage, 1566-1997', in P. Mavromoustakos (ed.), *Productions of Ancient Greek Drama in Europe during Modern Times*, 53-67. Athens: Kastaniotis.

E. Hall and F. Macintosh (2005), *Greek Tragedy and the British Theatre 1660-1914*. Oxford: Oxford UP.

M.R. Halleran (1985), *Stagecraft in Euripides*. London: Croom Helm.

W. Hift (1998), 'Euripides and the Damp Squib', *Scholia* 7, 72-81.

M. Hose (1990), *Studien zum Chor bei Euripides,* vol. 1. Stuttgart: Teubner.

M. Hose (1991), *Studien zum Chor bei Euripides,* vol. 2. Stuttgart: Teubner.

N.C. Hourmouziades (1965), *Production and Imagination in Euripides: Form and Function of the Scenic Space*. Athens: Athens UP.

G.O. Hutchinson (1985) (ed.), *Aeschylus: Seven Against Thebes*. Oxford: Clarendon Press.

J.J.F. de Jong (1991), *Narrative in Drama: The Art of the Euripidean Messenger-Speech*. Leiden: E.J. Brill.

J. Jouanna (1976), 'Texte et Espace Théâtrale dans les *Phéniciennes* d' Euripide', *Ktèma* 1, 81-97.

M. Kaimio (1988), *Physical Contact in Greek Tragedy: A Study of Stage Conventions*. Helsinki: Annales Academiae Scientiarum Fennicae.

J. Kamerbeek (1965), 'Prophecy and Tragedy', *Mnemosyne* 4, 29-40

Bibliography

A. Katsouris (1996), 'ΑΙΣΧΥΛΟΣ, ΕΠΤΑ ΕΠΙ ΘΗΒΑΣ', Dodone 25, 27-61.

G. Kerferd (1981), *The Sophistic Movement*. Cambridge: Cambridge UP.

J.C. Kosak (2004), *Heroic Measures: Hippocratic Medicine in the Making of Euripidean Tragedy*. Amsterdam: Brill.

D. Kovacs (1994), *Euripidea*. Leiden: Brill.

D. Kovacs (2002) (ed. and transl.), *Euripides: Helen, Phoenician Women, Orestes*. Cambridge, MA: Harvard UP.

D. Kovacs (2005), 'Text and Transmission', in J. Gregory (ed.), 379-93. Malden, MA and Oxford: Blackwell.

W. Kranz (1933), *Stasimon. Untersuchungen zu Form und Gehalt der griechischen Tragödie*. Berlin: Weidmann.

J. Kristeva (1969), *SÊMEIÔTIKÊ: Recherches pour une Sémanalyse*. Paris: Seuil.

J. Kristeva (1980), *Desire in Language. A Semiotic Approach to Literature and Art*, ed. L. Roudiez, transl. T. Gora, A. Jardine, L. Roudiez. NY: Columbia UP.

H. Kuch (1978), 'Zur Euripides-Rezeption im Hellenismus', *Klio* 60, 191-202.

M.R. Lefkowitz (1981), *The Lives of the Greek Poets*. Baltimore: The Johns Hopkins UP.

M.R. Lefkowitz (1987), 'Was Euripides an Atheist?', *Studi Italiani di Filologia Classica* 5, 149-65.

M. Lloyd (1992), *The Agon in Euripides*. Oxford: Clarendon Press.

C. Longo Rubbi (1967), 'La Danza "Magica" di Giocasta nelle *Fenicie* di Euripide', *Dioniso* 41, 398-409.

N. Loraux (1987), *Tragic Ways of Killing a Woman*, transl. A. Foster. Cambridge, MA: Harvard UP.

C.A.E. Luschnig (1995), *The Gorgon's Severed Head: Studies of Alcestis, Electra and Phoenissae*. Leiden: Brill.

F. Macintosh (1997), 'Tragedy in Performance: Nineteenth- and Twentieth-century Productions', in P.E. Easterling (ed.), 284-323. Cambridge: Cambridge UP.

A. D. Maingon (1989), 'Form and Content in the Lille Stesichorus', *Quaderni Urbinati di Cultura Classica* 31, 31-56.

J.P. March (1987), *The Creative Poet: Studies on the Treatment of Myths in Greek Poetry*. University of London: Institute of Classical Studies. Bulletin Supplement 49.

A. Masaracchia (1987), 'Ares nelle Fenicie di Euripide', in *Filologia e Forme Letterarie: Studi offerti à Francesco della Corte*, vol. 1, 169-81. Urbino: Università degli studi di Urbino.

D.J. Mastronarde (1984-5), 'Il Coro nelle *Fenicie* di Euripide: Una Testimonianza della Nuova Espressività Teatrale', *Dioniso* 55, 183-91. [Atti dell' XI Congresso Internazionale di Studi sul Teatro

Antico sul Tema 'Il Coro della Tragedia Greca: Struttura e Funzione'. Syracuse]

D.J. Mastronarde (1986), 'The Optimistic Rationalist in Euripides: Theseus, Jocasta, Teiresias', in M. Cropp, E. Fantham and S.E. Scully (eds), *Greek Tragedy and its Legacy: Essays Presented to D.J. Conacher*, 201-11. Calgary, Alberta: The University of Calgary Press.

D.J. Mastronarde (1988), *Phoenissae*. Leipzig: Teubner.

D.J. Mastronarde (1990), 'Actors on High: The Skênê Roof, the Crane, and the Gods in Attic Drama', *Classical Antiquity* 9, 247-94.

D.J. Mastronarde (1994), *Euripides: Phoenissae*. Cambridge: Cambridge UP.

D.J. Mastronarde (1998), 'Il Coro Euripideo: Autorità e Integrazione, *Quaderni Urbinati di Cultura Classica* n.s. 60, 3, 55-80.

D.J. Mastronarde and J.M. Bremer (1982), *The Textual Tradition of Euripides' Phoinissae*. Berkeley: University of California Classical Studies, 27.

P. Mavromoustakos et al. (1993), 'Performance History' in Κ. Τοπούζης (K. Topouzis), transl. *ΕΥΡΙΠΙΔΗΣ, ΦΟΙΝΙΣΣΑΙ*. Athens: Epikairotêta (Ancient Greek Theatre, 28), 199-224.

L. Méridier (1911), *Le Prologue dans la Tragédie d'Euripide*. Bordeaux: Feret.

J.D. Mikalson (1981), *Honor thy Gods: Popular Religion in Greek Tragedy*. Chapel Hill: University of North Carolina Press.

B. Morin (2001), 'La Séquence des Boucliers dans les *Phéniciennes* d'Euripide (vers 1104-40): Un Bestiaire Mythique au Service de l'Unité Athénienne?', *Revue des Études Grecques* 114, 37-83.

J. Mossman (2003) (ed.), *Euripides*. Oxford: Oxford UP.

M. Mueller (1980), *Children of Oedipus and Other Essays on the Imitation of Greek Tragedy 1550-1800*. Toronto: University of Toronto Press.

C. Mueller-Goldingen (1985), *Untersuchungen zu den Phönissen des Euripides*. Stuttgart: Franz Steiner.

C. Mueller-Goldingen (1995), 'Seneca und Euripides. Zur Rezeptionsgeschichte der *Phönissen*', *Rheinisches Museum* 138, 82-92.

A.S. Murray (1888), 'Illustrations of the *Phoenissae*', *Classical Review* 2, 327-28.

G. Murray (1909) (ed.), *Euripidis Fabulae*, III. Oxford: Oxford UP (Oxford Classical Texts).

E. Natanblut (2005), *The Seven against Thebes Myth in Greek Tragedy*. Montreal: Laodamia Press.

E.A.M.E. O'Connor Visser (1987), *Aspects of Human Sacrifice in the Tragedies of Euripides*. Amsterdam: B.R. Grüner.

N.F. O'Donnell (1954), 'A Lost Jacobean *Phoenissae*', *Modern Language Notes* 69, 163-4.

Bibliography

J.M. Osho (1977/78), 'Euripides' *Phoenissae* and Racine's *La Thèbaide*: A Comparative Analysis', *Museum Africum* 6, 82-93.

D.L. Page (1934), *Actors' Interpolations in Greek Tragedy*. Oxford: Clarendon Press.

H. Parry (1963), *The Choral Odes of Euripides: Problems of Structure and Dramatic Relevance*. (PhD Diss.) Berkeley: University of California.

P.J. Parsons (1977), 'The Lille "Stesichoros"', *Zeitschrift für Papyrologie und Epigraphik* 26, 7-36.

C. O. Pavese (1997), 'Sulla *Thebais* di Stesicoro', *Hermes* 125, 259-68.

C. Pelling (2005), 'Tragedy, Rhetoric, Performance', in J. Gregory (ed.), 83-102. Malden, MA and Oxford: Blackwell.

A.J. Podlecki (1962), 'Some Themes in Euripides' *Phoenissae*', *Transactions and Proceedings of the American Philological Association* 93, 355-73.

J.P. Poe (2000), '*Phoenissae* 88-201 and Pollux' ΔΙΣΤΕΓΙΑ', *Classical Philology* 95, 187-90.

A. Powell (1990) (ed.), *Euripides, Women and Sexuality*. London: Routledge.

J.U. Powell (1911) (ed.), *The Phoenissae of Euripides*. London: Constable & Company Ltd. [repr. 1979 by Arno Press]

N.S. Rabinowitz (1993), *Anxiety Veiled: Euripides and the Traffic in Women*. Ithaca, NY: Cornell UP.

R. Rehm (2002), *The Play of Space: Spatial Transformation in Greek Tragedy*. Princeton: Princeton UP.

R. Rehm (2003), *Radical Theatre: Greek Tragedy and the Modern World*. London: Duckworth.

J. Romilly, de (1965), 'Les *Phéniciennes* d' Euripide ou l' Actualité dans la Tragédie Grecque', *Revue de Philologie, de Littérature et d' Histoire Anciennes* 39, 28-47.

J. Romilly, de (1993), 'Le Rôle du Débat dans les *Phéniciennes* d' Euripide', in M. Glenn (ed.), *Philanthropia kai Eusebeia: Festschrift für Albrecht Dihle zum 70. Geburtstag*, 398-403. Göttingen: Pettersmann.

S. Saïd (1985), 'Euripide ou l' Attente Déçue: l' Example des *Phéniciennes*', *Annali della Scuola Normale Superiore di Pisa* 15, 501-27.

E. Scharffenberger (1995), 'A Tragic Lysistrata? Jocasta in the "Reconciliation Scene" of the *Phoenician Women*', *Rheinisches Museum* 138, 312-36.

R. Scodel (1997), 'Teichoskopia, Catalogue, and the Female Spectator in Euripides', *Colby Quarterly* 33, 76-93.

B. Seidensticker (1982), *Palintonos Harmonia: Studien zu komischen Elementen in der griechischen Tragödien*. Göttingen. Hypomnemata 72.

M.S. Silk (1996) (ed.), *Tragedy and the Tragic: Greek Theatre and Beyond*. Oxford: Clarendon Press.

J.P. Small (1981), *Studies Related to the Theban Cycle on Late Etruscan Urns*. Rome: Giorgio Bretschneider.

J.J. Smolenaars (1994), *Statius, Thebaid VII. A Commentary*. Leiden: Brill.

A.H. Sommerstein (2002), *Greek Drama and Dramatists*. London and New York: Routledge.

C. Sourvinou-Inwood (2003), *Tragedy and Athenian Religion*. Lanham: Lexington.

D.P. Stanley-Porter (1973), 'Mute Actors in the Tragedies of Euripides', *Bulletin of the Institute of Classical Studies* 20, 68-93.

P.T. Stevens (1976), 'Euripides and the Athenians', *Journal of Hellenic Studies* 76, 76-84.

I.C. Storey and A. Allan (2005), *A Guide to Ancient Greek Drama*. Malden, MA: Blackwell.

K. Synodinou (1977), *On the Concept of Slavery in Euripides*. Ioannina: Dodone.

O. Taplin (1977), *The Stagecraft of Aeschylus. The Dramatic Use of Exits and Entrances in Greek Tragedy*. Oxford: Oxford UP.

O. Taplin (1978), *Greek Tragedy in Action*. London: Routledge.

R.J. Tarrant (1978), 'Senecan Drama and its Antecedents', *Harvard Studies in Classical Philology* 82, 213-63.

W.G. Thalmann (1982), 'The Lille Stesichorus and the "Seven against Thebes" ', *Hermes* 110, 385-91.

D. Vessey (1973), *Statius and the Thebaid*. Cambridge: Cambridge UP.

F. Vian (1963), *Les origines de Thèbes*. Paris: Les Belles Lettres.

P. Walcot (1976), *Greek Drama in its Theatrical and Social Context*. Cardiff: University of Wales Press.

H.B. Walters (1894), 'Illustrations of Euripides' *Phoenissae*', *Classical Review* 8, 325-7.

R.W. Wallace (1998), 'The Sophists in Athens', in D. Boedeker and K.A. Raaflaub (eds), *Democracy, Empire, and the Arts in Fifth-century Athens,* 203-22. Cambridge, MA and London: Harvard UP.

T.B.L. Webster (1967), *The Tragedies of Euripides*. London: Methuen.

T.B.L. Webster (²1967), *Monuments illustrating Tragedy and Satyr Play*. Second edition, with Appendix. London: University of London (*Institute of Classical Studies*, 20).

T.B.L. Webster (1970), *The Greek Chorus*. London: Methuen.

T.B.L. Webster (²1970), *Greek Theatre Production*. London: Methuen.

U. Wilamowitz-Moellendorf, v. (1903), 'Der Schluss der *Phoenissen* des Euripides', *Sitzungsberichte der Preussischer Akademie der Wissenschaften*, 587-600.

D. Wiles (1997), *Tragedy in Athens. Performance Space and Theatrical Meaning*. Cambridge: Cambridge UP.

Bibliography

J. Wilkins (1990), 'The State and the Individual: Euripides' Plays of Voluntary Self-sacrifice', in A. Powell (ed.), 177-94. London & NY: Routledge.

C.W. Willink (1990), 'The Goddess EYΛABEIA and Pseudo-Euripides in Euripides' *Phoenissae*', *Proceedings of the Cambridge Philological Society* 216 (new series, no. 36), 182-201.

C.W. Willink (2002), 'The Invocations of Epaphus in Aeschylus, *Supplices* 40-57 and Euripides, *Phoenissae* 676-89', *Mnemosyne* 55, 711-18.

N. Wilson (1982), 'Observations on the *Lysistrata*', *Greek, Roman and Byzantine Studies* 23: 157-63.

P. Wilson (2005), 'Music', in J. Gregory (ed.), 183-93. Malden, MA and Oxford: Blackwell.

R.P. Winnington-Ingram (1969), 'Euripides: Poiêtês Sophos', *Arethusa* 2, 127-42. [repr. in J. Mossman (ed.), 47-63. Oxford: Oxford UP].

H. Yunis (1988), *A New Creed: Fundamental Religious Beliefs in the Athenian Polis and Euripidean Drama*. (Hypomnemata, 91). Göttingen: Vandenhoeck & Ruprecht.

F. Zeitlin (1982), *Under the Sign of the Shield: Semiotics and Aeschylus' Seven against Thebes*. Rome: Edizioni dell' Ateneo.

F. Zeitlin (1994), 'The Artful Eye: Vision, Ecphrasis and Spectacle in Euripidean Theatre', in S. Goldhill and R. Osborne (eds), *Art and Text in Euripidean Theatre*, 138-96. Cambridge: Cambridge UP.

B. Zimmermann (2001), 'Krieg und Frieden im Attischen Drama des 5. Jahrhunderts v. Chr.', *Hellenica* 51, 205-81.

G. Zuntz (1955), *The Political Plays of Euripides*. Manchester: Manchester UP.

Glossary of Ancient and Technical Terms

Agôn (pl. *agônes*). Contest, debate, festival.

Aposiopesis. Suppression of mention.

Deuteragonist. The second actor.

Exodos. Final scene of a tragedy, the part following the last choral ode.

Hypothesis (pl. *hypotheseis*). a preface to an ancient play.

Monody. Lyric song sung by a single actor.

Oikos. Household.

Orchêstra. 'Dancing place', the space at the centre of the performance area, between the stage and the spectators, where the Chorus performed.

Paidagogos. Tutor.

Parodos (pl. *parodoi*). Side-way (also called *eisodos*) leading into the *orchêstra* and also the first song of the Chorus.

Philos. Kin, friend.

Polis. City-state.

Prologos. Prologue, the opening part of the drama before the Chorus' entrance.

Protagonist. The first actor.

Skênê. Stage-building.

Scholium (pl. **scholia**). Ancient comment, a note written on the margins of a papyrus or a medieval manuscript.

Spartoi ('**Sown Men'**). The creatures which sprang from the earth following Cadmus' killing of the dragon and sowing of its teeth.

Stasimon (pl. *stasima*). 'Standing song(s)', choral ode(s) sung by the Chorus after they have entered during the *parodos* (q.v.) and taken their places in the *orchêstra* (q.v) and before the *exodos* (q.v.).

Strophe/antistrophe. Lyric passages which correspond to each other exactly in metre and style.

Teichoskopia. Viewing from the city walls.

Topos. Common element or repeated motif.

Tritagonist. The third actor.

Genealogical Table

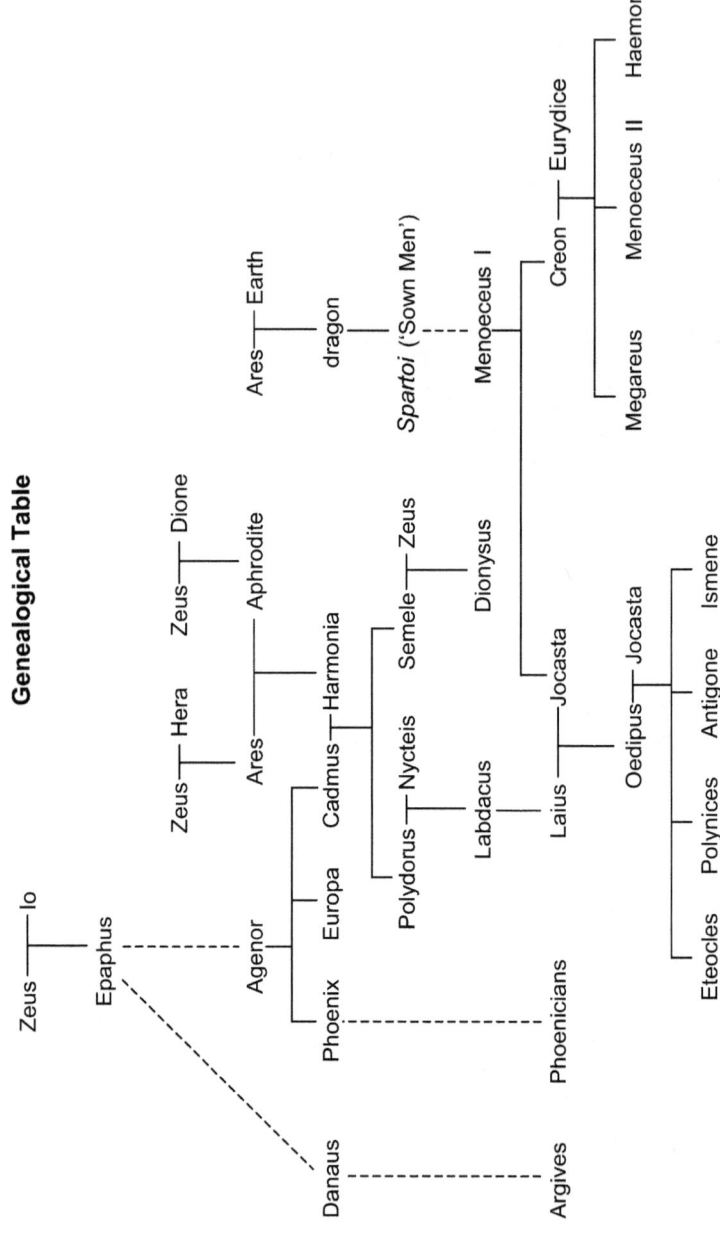

Chronology

BC
7th-6th cent.: Stesichorus
c. **6th cent.**: (epics) *Oedipodia* and *Thebaid*
6th cent.: Heracleitus
5th cent.: Strattis' *Phoenician Women*
c. **480**: Birth of Euripides
c. **476**: Phrynichus' victory with *Phoenician Women* (on Salamis)
467: Aeschylus' *Seven against Thebes*
455: Euripides' first production – third prize
441: Euripides' first victory (plays unknown)
438: Euripides' *Alcestis* – second prize
431: Outbreak of Peloponnesian War between Athens and Sparta
431: Euripides' *Medea* – third prize
c. **430-428**: Euripides' *Children of Heracles*
428: Euripides' *Hippolytus* (revised version) – first prize
c. **425**: Euripides' *Andromache*
before 423: Euripides' *Hecuba*
c. **424-420**: Euripides' *Suppliants*
c. **423**: Euripides' *Erechtheus*
c. **422-417**: Euripides' *Electra*
c. **422-415**: Euripides' *Heracles*
415: Disastrous Athenian expedition to Sicily (defeat in 413)
415: Euripides' *Trojan Women* (with *Alexander*, *Palamedes* and the satyr play *Sisyphus*) – second prize
415-10: Euripides' *Oedipus*
c. **414**: Euripides' *Iphigenia among the Taurians*
c. **413**: Euripides' *Ion*
412: Euripides' *Helen*
c. **412**: Euripides' *Cyclops* (satyr play)
411: Oligarchic regime of the Four Hundred at Athens
411: Aristophanes' *Women at the Thesmophoria*
411: Aristophanes' *Lysistrata*
c. **410**: Antimachus of Colophon, *Thebaid*
410-385: Aristophanes' *Phoenician Women* (fragmentary)
c. **409**: Euripides' *Phoenician Women*
408: Euripides' *Orestes*

408/7: Euripides goes to Macedonia
407/6: Death of Euripides
after 406: Euripides' *Bacchae* and *Iphigenia at Aulis* – first prize
405: Aristophanes' *Frogs*
404: Defeat of Athens by Sparta in the Peloponnesian War
401: Sophocles' *Oedipus at Colonus* (performed posthumously)
4th cent.: Lycurgus the orator
386: Regular revivals of tragedy introduced at the City Dionysia
c. **350**: Theatre of Epidaurus built
c. **330**: Aristotle's *Poetics*
330s: Reconstruction of Athenian theatre in stone by Lycurgus.
    Official records of Greek drama-texts established
3rd cent.: Satyrus, *Life of Euripides*
2nd cent.: Accius, *Phoenissae* (fragmentary)
195-180: Editions of Greek plays by Aristophanes of Byzantium
1st cent.: Ponticus, *Thebaid*
1st cent.: Diodorus of Sicily
1st cent.: Cicero

AD
1st cent.: Plutarch
1st cent.: Dio Chrysostom
1st cent.: Aulus Gellius
1st cent.: Lucan
1st cent.: Quintilianus
c. **62**: Seneca, *Phoenissae*
92: Statius, *Thebaid*
2nd cent.: Pausanias
2nd cent.: Lucian
2nd cent.: Suetonius
2nd-3rd cent.: Philostratus
3rd cent.: Athenaeus
3rd cent.: Dio Cassius
5th cent.: Stobaeus
10th cent.: Suda (Encyclopaedia)
14th cent.: Thomas Magister, *Life of Euripides*
1549: Lodovico Dolce, *Giocasta*
1601: G. Della Porta, *Gli duoi fratelli rivali*
1618: T. Goffe, *The Courageous Turk*
1723: J. Robe, *The Fatal Legacy*
1803: F. Schiller, *Die Braut von Messina*
1821: *Ion*. Adaptation (based on Euripides' *Hippolytus, Ion, Phoenician Women* and Sophocles' *Antigone, Oedipus the King, Oedipus at Colonus* and *Trachiniae*) by Thomas Talfourd. Great Britain and USA

1890: *Phoenizierinnen*. Directed by Ludwig Barnay. Germany
1904: *Phoinissai*. Directed by Thomas Oikonomou. Greece
1927: *Phoenician Maidens*. Occidental College (Department of Greek), USA
1934: *Phoinissai*. Directed by Linos Karzis. Greece
1938: *Phoinissai*. Directed by Linos Karzis. Greece
1941: *Phoinissai*. Directed by Linos Karzis. Greece
1948: *Phoinissai*. Directed by Linos Karzis. Greece
1960: *Phoinissai*. Directed by Alexis Minotis. Greece
1961: *Phoinissai*. Directed by Linos Karzis. Greece
1961: *Phoinissae*. Radley College, Oxfordshire, Great Britain
1962: *Le Fenicie*. Directed by Franco Enriquez. Italy
1965: *Phoinissai*. Directed by Linos Karzis. Greece
1967: *The Phoenician Women*. Directed by David Thompson. Great Britain
1968: *Le Fenicie*. Directed by Franco Enriquez. Italy
1971: *Phoinissai*. Directed by Thanos Kotsopoulos. Greece
1977: *The Sons of Oedipus*. Directed by David Thompson. London
1978: *Phoinissai*. Directed by Alexis Minotis. Greece
1979: *Phoinissai*. Directed by Stavros Doufexis. Greece
1981: *Phoenizierinnen*. Directed by Hansgünther Heyme. Germany
1982: *Les Phéniciennes*. Directed by Michel Deutsch and Philippe Lacoue-Labarthe. France
1983: *Phoinissai*. Directed by Leonidas Trivizas. Greece
1987: *Oi Teleutaies Poleis* ('The Last Cities'). An adaptation based on Euripides' *Phoenician Women* and Herodas' *Mimiambs*. Directed by I. Chouvardas. Greece
1987 (performance): Symphony No 5 by Mikis Theodorakis (composer) (based on Aeschylus' *Eumenides* and Euripides' *Phoenician Women*)
1988: *Phoinissai*. Directed by Alexis Minotis. Greece
1990: Euripides' *Phoinissai*. Directed by N. Charalabous. Cyprus
1991: *Euripides' Phoenissae and The Dukes of Hazzard*. Parody. USA
1993: *Tanguedia*. Directed by Kristi Wilson. USA
1994: *OMMA: Oedipus and the Luck of Thebes*. Directed by Tim Supple. Great Britain
1995-6: *Phoenician Women*. Directed by Katie Mitchell. Great Britain
1996: *Fenicische Vrouwen*. Directed by Johan Simons. The Netherlands
1997: *Le Fenicie*. Directed by Gabriele Vacis. Italy
1997: *Phoinisses*. Directed by Ioannis Karachisaridis. Greece
1998: *Fenicie*. Directed by Francesca Nenci. Italy
1999: *Phoinisses*. Directed by N. Chourmouziades. Greece
1999 (performance): *Antigone*. Opera. Mikis Theodorakis (composer)

2000: *Phoenician Women*. Directed by Mark Oldknow
2002: *The Phoenician Women*. Directed by Steven Little. Great Britain
2002: *The Phoenician Women*. Directed by David Travis. Great Britain
2003: *Phoenician Women*. Clifton College, Bristol, Great Britain
2003: *Thebans*. Adaptation by Liz Lochhead, based on Euripides' *Phoenician Women* and Sophocles' *Antigone* and *Oedipus the King*. Directed by Graham McLaren. Great Britain
2004: *Post-Oedipus*. Directed by Steven Gridley. USA
2006: *Phoenician Women*. Directed by Bob Bartlett. USA

Index

www.ingramcontent.com/pod-product-compliance
Lightning Source LLC
Chambersburg PA
CBHW050408030726
47503CB00006B/2084